in 3 easy steps

easy steps *conrad gallagher*

food without the fuss

To Candy and my soon to be born child...
With love, I wait

First published in Great Britain 2005 by
Kyle Cathie Limited
122 Arlington Road
London NW1 7HP
general.enquiries@kyle-cathie.com
www.kylecathie.com

10 9 8 7 6 5 4 3

ISBN 1 85626 572 2

Senior Editor Kyle Cathie
Design and art direction Geoff Hayes
Photography Gus Filgate
Home economy Conrad Gallagher and Annie Nichols
Styling Penny Markham
Copy editor Sophie Allen
Production Sha Huxtable and Alice Holloway
All photographs by Gus Filgate except pp. 48, 120, Martin Brigdale; 58, 83, 153, Georgia
Glynn Smith; 100, Will Heap

A Cataloguing In Publication record for this title is available from the British Library.
Colour reproduction by Sang Choy
Printed and bound by Star Standard

contents

introduction 06

starters and soups 12

fish 42

meat and poultry   66

pasta and risottos 96

vegetables 108

desserts 122

index 158

introduction

'Sophisticated yet uncomplicated' – these recipes have been devised with this very mantra in mind... and I wanted to make beautifully presented and delicious tasting food without causing a daytime of shopping or an afternoon of cooking.

In 3 Easy Steps was inspired by the great response to my previous books, *One Pot Wonders* and *Take 6 Ingredients*; in the first book washing up kept to a minimum, in the second, shopping is minimal. I wanted to create recipes in the same vein, that were 'user-friendly' and accessible in the most ordinary of kitchens. As always, I encourage you to choose the finest and freshest ingredients possible (the basis for any great meal) and prepare them without fuss for guaranteed success. I hope to illustrate this principal throughout this book. With the use of simple equipment, limited work surfaces and easy techniques, the introduction of 3 easy stages to prepare each flavourful dish was created.

The focus in the recipes is always to use produce of the finest quality, as seasonally fresh ingredients always set the stage for a great-tasting dish. Less is always more and, by buying better produce, less needs to be done to the ingredients, thus allowing the natural flavours to work by themselves, adding to the great flavour of the dish as nature intended it to be. Wherever you live, it is important to take the time to seek out stores stocked with the best produce you can afford, as well as top-quality prepared foods. Good, basic cooking techniques play an important role too, making it easy for you to execute each recipe effectively. Making cooking fun is my main criterion. Also I want to knock on the head the myth that entertaining is time consuming

In the fast-paced world in which we live, with the constant need to fit more into daily life, to be more time-efficient, and to make communication faster through technology, I strongly feel that entertaining should be a vital part. Most importantly, entertaining is for relaxation purposes. Being creative with food, and fundamentally to enjoy life with the people closest to you by sharing a gorgeous meal, prepared with ease and presented with style, is one of life's joys. I for one have a hectic schedule and am constantly on the move, so making gourmet meals without the hassle is a constant for me. I have always maintained that spending less time in the kitchen and more quality time with loved ones is essential.

Because entertaining is all about the people, and whom you choose to surround yourself by, why not include your guests in the making of the meal? In my experience, guests always feel more important being given a job or task to do, and feel good about having contributed to the end result, and therefore minimise the host's time spent in the kitchen.

An open kitchen always lends nicely to this idea, as guests may come and go, sipping wine and casually wandering in and out of the room to watch you put cooking in 3 easy steps into practice. Encourage guests to help themselves to wine and participate in offering the pre-dinner snacks around. After all, your guests have not come to mingle aimlessly in your lounge, but rather to spend an evening with you, their host, and if that means having to put some creativity in themselves, either by putting the table setting together or dressing the salad, so be it.

An open plan kitchen allows you to have fun with dining and gives you a chance to interact with your guests without being hoarded in a closed-off room, sweating and panicking that you cannot be in two places at once. I hope I have reduced the time spent in the kitchen but cutting out unnecessary steps; the hassle and strain of peeling, chopping and sealing have been reduced. My techniques aim to leave the cook in a state of relaxation, confident that the easy procedures will lead to a perfect gourmet meal, having had a good time preparing it and boasting the ease of doing it! Presentation always adds to compliment a meal, so use your own creative edge along with my suggestions and remember the more simple the idea, the more potent the effect will be.

Because this type of cooking lends itself to being effortless and elegant, the cleaning up should follow suit, thus I have kept cooking equipment to an absolute minimum.

With each recipe, you find yourself not having to spend time in preparing the ingredients, as the superb ingredients you have chosen work naturally by themselves, and the simple procedures allow you to enjoy the evening as well as conduct it, as each cooking stage flows progressively.

The host's temperament will always set the stage for the feel and tempo of the evening, therefore straining and exhausting yourself in the kitchen will not be conducive to the mood. Where a frustrated burnt-out cook will create a feeling of pressure and haste, a relaxed and calm host will induce chatting and festivities of the guests to colour the occasion.

By using non-complex recipes, the margin for error is greatly reduced, allowing you to focus more on the occasion itself. *In 3 Easy Steps* focuses on this very principle. It also highlights my love for combinations of subtle flavours.

If there are stages you can prepare beforehand, always take advantage of this, as then you have more time for last minute attention to the meal itself. To mark a special occasion, prepare a drink that is individual to the occasion, like my Iced Pomegranate Jelly Shots... a pure party indulgence!

From Shepherd's Pie cooked with Beer to Lobster drizzled with Cardamom, Chocolate and Orange, I hope you find as many excuses possible to entertain and test the eclectic mix of recipes in this book.

Have fun, cook simply, eat well.

cooking notes

A few unusual ingredients

Banana leaves - use them to wrap foods; they hold in the moisture and impart an aromatic flavour during cooking. Available in African, Asian and Middle Eastern stores.

Cane sugar – less refined than granulated white sugar, it is sticky and the taste is closer to that of sugar cane.

Cape Malay spice – is a combination of allspice, aniseed, fennel seeds, fenugreek, bay, cardamom, turmeric, curry leaves, cinnamon, clove, ginger, garlic, mustard seeds, naartjie peel, nutmeg and saffron. It is used as a seasoning for stews and to flavour meats and even sometimes desserts.

Courgette flowers – buy them while the flower is still closed and with no brown, dry bits obvious. Kept in the refrigerator they will last up to 3 days. Available from good vegetable shops and local markets.

Drunken pecorino – cheese that has been marinated in alcohol; available from Italian delicatessens.

Duck eggs – have a faint taste of duck meat and are very rich, perfect for baking and for making omelettes. Buy organic duck eggs from a good farmer.

Green papaya - is a raw/unripened papaya. It has a mild almost bland taste and is usually served grated. Season with hot and sour spice. It also picks up salty flavours.

High-grown melon - this just means that it has been grown at a high altitude which increases the quality of the fruit.

Mustard seeds – come in black (spicy and piquant), yellow (less piquant) and white (a little bitter and pungent). Use them whole or in ground form. Widely available in supermarkets and Asian stores.

Mirin - a Japanese spirit-based liquid sweetener that is used only for cooking, usually in marinades, glazes and simmered dishes.

Nori – edible, scented seaweed from Japan. Several varieties grow along the coastline. Nori is available as powder, in strands, and as whole, pressed and dried sheets. It can also be bought sweetened, flavoured with saké or soy.

Piri piri – a hot chilli and capsicum sauce originating from Portugal. The heat can be controlled by the amount of chilli added. Available in supermarkets in bottled form.

Saké - a Japanese alcoholic drink, that is familiar wherever there are Japanese restaurants. It is usually drunk as a 'rice wine' , but in Japan it is an important culinary ingredient for tenderising and toning down saltiness. It can also be used for pickling purposes.

Squab – is young pigeon and available wild or farmed. Wild squab has denser meat and is more full of flavour than farmed birds.

hollandaise sauce

A handy recipe to have. Please use for the recipes on page 18.

3 tablespoons water
500g (18oz) clarified butter, melted
5 egg yolks
1/2 lemon
Pinch of salt and white pepper

Warm the water in a bowl sitting over a pan of hot water. Whisk the egg yolks and seasoning in the pan with the water until the consistency of thick cream. Carry on whisking and start adding the liquid butter in a slow steady stream until glossy and thick. Add in the lemon juice and adjust the seasoning.

caesar dressing

Please use for the recipe on page 33.

1 egg
2 tablespoons white wine vinegar
2 tablespoons Dijon mustard
2 minced anchovy fillets
1 teaspoon garlic purée
150ml (5fl oz) olive oil
Sea salt and freshly ground black pepper

Boil the egg for 1 minute and break it into a bowl. Add all the ingredients except the olive oil and whisk together. Add the olive oil in a slow and steady stream until all combined and smooth.

tomato fondue

This is such a useful staple to have in the fridge. Please use for the recipes on pages 59, 87, 98 and 114.

1 tablespoon olive oil
4 shallots, finely chopped
2 garlic cloves, crushed
8 plum tomatoes, skinned, deseeded and chopped
1 thyme sprig
1 rosemary sprig
1 tablespoon tomato purée
Salt and pepper

Heat the oil in a pan over a moderate heat and sweat the shallots and garlic until soft but not coloured. Add the tomatoes, herbs and tomato purée. Simmer gently until the liquid has all evaporated and the mixture is quite dry. Season well and allow to cool. Refrigerate until ready to use.

starters and soups

figs wrapped in **jambon de bayonne** with ricotta and sugar cane

This ham is gorgeously French and has been rubbed with a special salt and herb mix – a recipe that has been passed down many generations. The ham is hung and dried for 180 days, which provides it with its signature taste.

SERVES 4

8 slices of Jambon de
  Bayonnne, sliced
  lengthways
16–20 figs, scored at the top
  and slightly squeezed out
4 tablespoons ricotta cheese
1 medium piece of sugar
  cane, finely grated
4 tablespoons wild honey

1 Wrap the ham around the open figs and spoon the ricotta into the opening of each fig.

2 Sprinkle the grated cane sugar on top of the cheese and place under a hot grill until the figs are warm and the cheese starts to brown slightly.

3 Drizzle with wild honey and serve immediately.

foie gras with sauternes and apple purée

A classic serving of foie gras calls for a classic accompaniment such as the sweet white wine Sauternes. Instead of serving the wine with the foie gras I have chosen to use it in the cooking process and serve it as a sauce.

SERVES 4

2 Granny Smith apples, peeled
Sugar syrup
4 good slices of foie gras
125ml (4fl oz) Sauternes
8 thyme sprigs
Salt and pepper

1 Boil the apples in a little sugar syrup and, when soft, strip out the cores and purée the flesh. Arrange 3 small spoonfuls of the purée on each warmed serving plate.

2 Heat a non-stick frying pan until it is very hot. Sear the foie gras for no longer than 30 seconds on each side. Place the foie gras slices beside the apple purée.

3 Deglaze the pan with the Sauternes, season, then drizzle the sauce over the foie gras. Garnish with the thyme.

roasted beetroot with **crab meat** and curried crème fraîche

Baby beetroots are a lot sweeter than their larger counterparts. They are easy to grow and taste even better straight from your garden. Remember to scrub them well to remove any traces of soil.

SERVES 4

12 baby beetroots, washed
3 oregano sprigs
30ml (1fl oz) balsamic vinegar
Salt and pepper

For the crème fraîche:
1 shallot, finely chopped
1 stick (about 2.5cm/1 in) of ginger, peeled and grated
1 garlic clove, finely chopped
1 teaspoon curry powder
100ml (3½fl oz) crème fraîche
Olive oil

300g (10½oz) cooked crab meat
30ml (1fl oz) fresh lemon juice
2 teaspoons chopped parsley
Long, fresh chives to garnish

1 Wrap the beetroots, with oregano, balsamic vinegar and seasoning, in tinfoil, and roast in a preheated oven at 180ºC/350ºF/gas 4 for 45 minutes or until done. Peel and halve them.

2 Fry the shallot, ginger, garlic and curry powder over a low heat in some olive oil. Remove after 10 minutes and let it cool. Stir in the crème fraîche and refrigerate.

3 Add the crab, lemon and parsley to the crème fraîche. Layer into a pastry cutter, alternating with the beetroot. Remove the cutter and garnish with chives.

eggs benedict with **chorizo**

Instead of using traditional ham or bacon, use chorizo to give it a kick in the right direction.

SERVES 4

4 eggs

1 chorizo sausage, sliced

4 English muffins, cut in half and lightly toasted

4 tablespoons Hollandaise sauce (see pages 10-11)

1 Poach the eggs and spoon onto kitchen paper.

2 Pan-fry the chorizo and place on the muffins.

3 Place the poached eggs on the chorizo and smother with Hollandaise.

eggs benedict with **serrano ham** and crispy sage

This is the ultimate breakfast and brunch food – and one of my all-time favourites. I have to say the best I have ever tasted had to be in New York, where it originated. You can use more than one slice of Serrano ham if you're feeling generous, and serve it on the side.

SERVES 4

4 thin slices of Serrano ham

4 sage leaves

Olive oil

2 English muffins, cut in half and lightly toasted

4 eggs

4 tablespoons Hollandaise sauce (see pages 10-11)

Salt and pepper

1 Fry the Serrano ham and sage leaves in some olive oil until crispy and put the ham on the muffins.

2 Poach the eggs and place on the ham and season.

3 Spoon on the Hollandaise and garnish with the crispy sage.

drunken **pecorino** salad with serrano ham, tapenade and high-grown melon

Pecorino is an Italian ewes' milk cheese which is hard pressed and grainy with a yellow crust when mature. The name is derived from the Italian word for ewe, *pecora*. If you are ever in Italy make sure you try the real thing. Serrano ham is somewhat different from Parma ham, but still great to have with melon – an excellent and refreshing combination!

SERVES 4

450g (1lb) mixed salad
  greens
1 medium melon, sliced
  into 16 thin wedges
20 chives, roughly chopped
1 bunch of parsley, leaves
  picked
1 bunch of chervil, leaves
  picked
24 thin slices of Serrano ham
225g (8oz) drunken
  pecorino, shaved
Freshly ground pepper
Coarse sea salt
50g (2oz) olive tapenade
3 tablespoons olive oil

1 Arrange the salad leaves in wide-rim bowls, then place the melon wedges on top. Sprinkle some of the herbs over the melon.

2 Fold the ham into rosettes and place them on top of the salad. Scatter over the cheese, remaining herbs and season.

3 Mix the tapenade with the olive oil and dress the salad.

snails stuffed with ginger, lemongrass, coconut and coriander butter

This is a real fusion dish with French and Thai influences. Try my variation to the traditional garlic butter and croûtons.

SERVES 4

200g (7oz) soft butter
15g (^{2}/3oz) ginger, grated
15g (^{2}/3oz) lemongrass,
  grated
15g (^{2}/3oz) coconut, grated
1 small bunch of coriander,
  chopped
1 garlic clove, finely
  chopped
48 snails, cooked and shells
  sterilised in boiling salted
  water
Salt and pepper

1 Mix all the ingredients together except the snails.

2 Place a little of the butter mixture in the bottom of each shell, insert the snail and then cover with more butter.

3 Arrange in snail dishes and put in a preheated oven at 180ºC/350ºF/gas 4 until the butter starts to bubble.

roasted **prawns** with piri-piri

Piri-piri originated in Portugal and was introduced to Africa over 400 years ago. I like it hot, especially if it makes my eyes water. Use it as a basting, a marinade or as a condiment. Serve with warm crusty bread to dip into the leftover juices.

SERVES 4

2 chillies
4 tablespoons lime juice
4 tablespoons vegetable oil
1 tablespoon cayenne pepper
1 garlic clove, chopped
1 small bunch of dill, chopped
1 teaspoon salt
1 teaspoon freshly ground pepper
20 large prawns

1 Mix all the ingredients, except the prawns, in a food processor until smooth.

2 Marinate the prawns in the sauce overnight.

3 Remove from the fridge and cook under a hot grill for 5 minutes or until done.

mussels steamed in mild apple cider with sour cream and oregano

Mussels are child's play to cook. They are really easy to gather from the rocks and nothing can beat the satisfaction of cooking mussels that you have picked yourself.

SERVES 4

150ml (5fl oz) cider
1.3kg (3lb) fresh mussels,
　scrubbed and bearded
100ml (3¹/₂fl oz) sour cream
8 fresh oregano sprigs,
　leaves picked
Juice of ¹/₂ lemon
Salt and pepper

1　Place the cider in a large pan and bring to the boil. Add the mussels and steam for 5 minutes or until the mussels have opened. Discard any that remain closed. Strain and reserve the cooking liquid.

2　Bring the cooking liquid to the boil, then stir in the sour cream and oregano and season.

3　Add the mussels to the sauce and warm through. Check the seasoning and add the lemon. Spoon into deep bowls and serve.

sautéed frogs legs in parsley and ginger butter

Compound butters are easy to make yet extremely versatile. For this recipe use fresh ginger as opposed to dried which would overpower the subtle flavour of the frogs legs.

SERVES 4

110g (4oz) unsalted butter
1 stick (about 2.5cm/ 1 in) of
　fresh ginger, peeled and
　grated
50g (2oz) flat-leaf parsley,
　chopped
20 pairs of frogs legs
Salt and pepper

1　Mix the butter, ginger and parsley until well combined.

2　Heat a heavy-based pan and fry the frogs legs in the butter mixture.

3　Season the mixture and arrange in deep bowls and spoon the butter over as the sauce.

tempura of **prawns**, braised chicory, chilli and lime

I love the sweetness of the prawns and the bitterness of the chicory; together a great combination. Tempura is the perfect light batter and using ice-cold sparkling water is essential for a superior outcome.

SERVES 4

150ml (5fl oz) vegetable oil
50ml (2fl oz) ice-cold
**   sparkling water**
100g (3¹/₂oz) tempura flour
16 large prawns, shells
**   removed**
Flour for dusting
3 large heads of chicory,
**   quartered**
Olive oil
Zest and juice of 1 lime
3 chillies, seeded and cut
**   into julienne strips**
Salt and pepper

1 Mix the water and tempura together and rest for 10 minutes. Meanwhile, dust the prawns with flour, season and then dip into the rested batter.

2 Deep-fry in the vegetable oil until golden. Remove and drain onto kitchen paper.

3 Braise the chicory in olive oil, arrange 3 pieces on each plate and drizzle juices over and around. Place the prawns on top, sprinkle with the lime juice and scatter chilli and lime zest around them.

tempura of **sole**, sesame seed and mary rose sauce

Insist on fresh sole from your fishmonger. It will make all the difference to the taste.

SERVES 4

125ml (4fl oz) home-made
**   mayonnaise**
125ml (4fl oz) good tomato
**   ketchup**
1 teaspoon Worcestershire
**   sauce**
1 teaspoon Tabasco sauce
30ml (1fl oz) brandy
200g (7oz) tempura flour
1 teaspoon white sesame
**   seeds**
1 teaspoon black sesame
**   seeds**
125ml (4fl oz) cold sparkling
**   mineral water**
4 soles, skinned and filleted
Flour for dusting
150ml (5fl oz) vegetable oil
4 Lemon wedges
Baby red chard, wilted
Salt and pepper

1 Mix the mayonnaise, ketchup, Worcestershire sauce, Tabasco and brandy together. Season and refrigerate.

2 Season the tempura flour with salt, pepper and the sesame seeds and mix in the cold water. Rest in a cool place for 10 minutes.

3 Dust the sole fillets with flour, dip in the batter and deep-fry in the vegetable oil until lightly golden. Drain on kitchen paper and serve on top of the sauce and baby red chard and garnish with a lemon wedge. Sprinkle sesame seeds around the plate.

tartare of **eel**

Whatever their origin or exterior appearance, eels are widely popular in Europe and Japan, where many consider their rich, sweet, firm meat a delicacy.

SERVES 4

2 whole eels, skinned, gutted
   and deboned
1/2 cucumber, peeled and
   seeded, finely diced
1/2 red pepper, seeded and
   finely diced
2 tablespoons capers,
   chopped
2 plum tomatoes, skinned,
   seeded and finely diced
15 chives, finely chopped
4 chervil sprigs
Salt and pepper

1 Chop the eels very finely. Season them with salt and pepper.

2 Mix the eel with the rest of the ingredients, except the chervil, and spoon into 4 ring moulds or pastry cutters.

3 Place on plates, remove the ring moulds and garnish with the chervil.

three **squid** rings in nori and polenta dust

Nori sheets are used in the preparation of sushi. Here nori is used for dusting the squid. It has such a distinct flavour and can be purchased from any good food store. Polenta adds a contrasting crispy crunch to the succulent squid rings.

SERVES 4

4 nori sheets
50g (2oz) polenta
12 squid rings
50g (2oz) seasoned flour
2 eggs, beaten
150ml (5fl oz) vegetable oil
1 lemon, segmented
4 large chervil sprigs

1 Blend the nori sheets and polenta in a food processor until really fine like dust.

2 Dust the squid rings in the seasoned flour and dip in the egg. Roll in the nori/polenta crust and deep-fry in the vegetable oil.

3 Place in a circle and garnish with the lemon wedges and chervil.

oysters with nori, cucumber, radish and ossetra caviar

Always buy your oysters alive with the shells closed. Oysters are easy to open once you know how, but ask your fishmonger to do it if you are a little unsure. Turn the flesh over and ensure that there are no splinters.

SERVES 4

1 lemon, cut in half
100ml (3¹/₂fl oz) grapeseed oil
30ml (1fl oz) rice wine vinegar
Mirin to taste
1kg (21/4lb) rock salt
50g (2oz) pink peppercorns
20 chives, chopped very thinly
24 oysters, opened and the juice reserved
4 red radishes, well washed and cut into fine julienne
¹/₂ cucumber, peeled, seeded and cut into small brinoise
4 teaspoons ossetra caviar
20g (3/4oz) chervil
2 sheets of nori, cut from one corner to the other, rolled into a cone
Pepper

1 Marinate the lemon in the oil overnight. Next day, squeeze the juice into the oil, add the rice wine vinegar, oyster juice and mirin to taste, and season with pepper.

2 Mix the rock salt, peppercorns and chives. Divide and place in the centre of 4 large plates, flattening into a circle. Arrange 6 oysters on the salt and garnish each with a little radish, cucumber, caviar and a tiny piece of chervil. Spoon in a little dressing.

3 Place the nori cone in the centre of the oysters and fill with a bit of radish and the remainder of the chervil.

stuffed mediterranean **courgette** flowers

Courgette flowers are not just pretty, they are extremely versatile and you can stuff them with almost anything.

SERVES 4

1 red pepper, seeded and cut
  into small dice
1 yellow pepper, seeded and
  cut into small dice
1 shallot, finely chopped
2 garlic cloves, crushed and
  finely chopped
50g (2oz) black olives, seeded
  and chopped
1 small bunch of basil, leaves
  picked and chopped
16 courgette flowers, washed
  3 times
50g (2oz) flour
2 eggs, beaten
100g (3½oz) fresh
  breadcrumbs
150ml (5fl oz) vegetable oil
Salt and pepper

1   Mix the peppers, shallot, garlic, olives and basil together, season, and stuff the flowers with the mixture.

2   Dust the flowers in flour, dip them in the egg and then the breadcrumbs.

3   Deep-fry in the vegetable oil until golden.

simple caesar **salad**

As the heading says, simple. A fast meal to which you can add anything from fish to poached eggs, and even meat strips.

SERVES 4

4 heads of baby cos lettuce
8 long chives, blanched
4 slices of white bread,
  preferably ciabatta,
  crôuton-sized
250ml (9fl oz) clarified
  butter
1 garlic clove, crushed and
  finely chopped
150g (5oz) freshly grated
  Parmesan
8 slices of pancetta, crisped
  up in the oven
1 recipe Caesar dressing (see
  page 10-11)

1   Wash the lettuce and tie them into 4 equal bundles with the chives.

2   Fry the bread in clarified butter until crisp and toss in the garlic and a little of the Parmesan.

3   Garnish each lettuce bundle with the croûtons, grated cheese, pancetta and dressing.

truffle scrambled **duck egg** with brioche and nut vinaigrette

This is the ultimate in richness. Duck eggs are tastier than chicken eggs. Adding the truffle just enhances the richness, and serving it with a luxury bread, like brioche, is just sinfully divine.

SERVES 4

1 tablespoon white wine
   vinegar
3 tablespoons nut oil
2 teaspoons truffle oil
4 tablespoons clarified
   butter
4 duck eggs, whisked
50ml (2fl oz) double cream
15 chives, finely chopped
10 slices of fresh truffles, 6
   finely diced
4 slices of fresh brioche,
   buttered
Salt and pepper

1 Make the nut vinaigrette by mixing the vinegar, nut oil and truffle oil and seasoning.

2 In a hot non-stick pan, heat the clarified butter and add the egg mix. Continually stir with a rubber spatula and add the cream, chives and finely diced truffles. Season.

3 Spoon the egg over the brioche, then place the truffle slices on top and finish with the nut vinaigrette.

sautéed calf **sweetbreads** with gorgonzola and red onions

Prized by gourmets throughout the world, this delicacy can be used in fillings and ragoûts and is a reputable delicacy. Serve with a green salad and crusty bread.

SERVES 4

75ml (3fl oz) olive oil
400g (14oz) calf sweetbreads,
   cubed
4 red onions, diced
2 garlic cloves, finely
   chopped
125ml (4fl oz) white wine
7g (¼oz) thyme, chopped
50g (2oz) Gorgonzola cheese
Salt and pepper

1 Heat a heavy-based frying pan and add the olive oil. Sauté the sweetbreads until they are golden; add the onions, and then the garlic and cook until softened.

2 Deglaze the pan with the white wine, add the thyme and cook for 15 minutes until the sauce thickens slightly.

3 Add the cheese and stir in, check the seasoning and place under a preheated hot grill to gratinate for a few minutes and then serve.

beetroot and cumin dip with gherkins

This versatile dip could be served at a summer cocktail party or around a warm fire in the heart of winter. It is both refreshing and comforting. Not only is it good, but very easy to prepare. Serve with good crusty bread.

SERVES 4

4 large beetroots
Olive oil
**1 teaspoon toasted cumin
  seeds, ground**
4 garlic cloves
150ml (5fl oz) crème fraîche
Salt and pepper
Gherkins
**2 teaspoons toasted cumin
seeds, for garnish**

1 Roast the beetroots with olive oil, seasoning, cumin and garlic in a preheated oven at 180ºC/350ºF/gas 4 for approximately 45 minutes or until soft.

2 Peel and purée the beetroot with the garlic until smooth.

3 Spoon onto a serving plate, dollop the crème fraîche on top and serve with gherkins and garnish with a few cumin seeds.

avocado stuffed with giant prawns, avocado cream and pink grapefruit

A twist of the classical Avocado Ritz. Prepare this beforehand so you can spend more time with your guests.

SERVES 4

**6 avocados, 4 cut in half
  with the stone removed**
2 tablespoons crème fraîche
Juice of 2 lemons
**16 giant prawns, peeled and
  deveined**
**2 large pink grapefruits,
segmented**
Salt and pepper

1 Blend the flesh of 2 avocados with the crème fraîche and half the lemon juice until smooth. Season and pour the rest of the lemon juice on top.

2 In a hot sauté pan, sauté the prawns until they are just cooked and season. Cool until needed.

3 Just before serving, place 2 prawns into each halved avocado, spoon the avocado cream over the prawns and garnish with the grapefruit segments.

real french **onion** soup with gruyère

The secret of a good onion soup is to slowly caramelise the onion to maximise the flavours and colour. Whenever I find myself in France, French onion soup is at the top of my list.

SERVES 4

2 tablespoons olive oil
20g (³/₄oz) butter
300g (10¹/₂oz) white onions, finely sliced
25g (1oz) flour
2 litres (3¹/₂ pints) good, white chicken or vegetable stock, flavoured with 2 tablespoons Madeira
8 thyme sprigs, leaves picked
4 slices of French loaf, rubbed with a garlic clove
50g (2oz) grated Gruyère
Salt and pepper

1 Heat the olive oil and butter in a thick-based pan and caramelise the onions over a low heat for 30 minutes.

2 Add the flour and cook for 5 minutes. Pour in the flavoured stock, thyme leaves and seasoning and cook for 30 minutes.

3 Serve piping hot with the Gruyère melted on top and the slices of French loaf.

saffron broth with pepper-stuffed baby **squid** and green tomatoes

A soup is only as good as its stock. It is therefore vital that you use only the best stock for this broth. If not, even a special ingredient, like saffron, cannot save it.

SERVES 4

1 oven-roasted red pepper, (180°C/350°F/mark 4 for 15 minutes) peeled and chopped
2 tablespoons chopped parsley
8 baby squid tubes, cleaned and rinsed
600ml (1 pint) strong, clear chicken stock
1g saffron
1 green tomato, sliced
1 teaspoon caster sugar
Salt and pepper

1 Mix the pepper and parsley, season, and stuff the squid tubes with the mixture.

2 Bring the stock to a rapid boil, add the saffron and season well. Add the squid and cook for 7 minutes.

3 Caramelise the tomato with the caster sugar over a medium heat and add to the soup.

cauliflower and cumin soup with seared **scallops**

Adding cumin to the cauliflower soup does spice things up! This combination is perfect for a chilly winter's day.

SERVES 4

4 shallots, chopped
2 garlic cloves, crushed
2 teaspoons ground cumin
2 heads of cauliflower, stalks removed and cut into florets
Olive oil
400ml (14fl oz) chicken stock
100ml (3^1/$_2$fl oz) double cream
8 medium scallops
Small knob of butter
Salt and pepper

1 Sweat the shallots, garlic, cumin and cauliflower in olive oil for 7 minutes. Add the chicken stock and bring to the boil. Cook until the cauliflower is just tender.

2 Purée the soup and add the cream. Strain through a conical strainer and season.

3 Sear the scallops in a hot pan with the butter, season and add to the soup.

cold avocado soup with avocado and **oyster** tartare

This soup is rich and creamy. It is a light summer meal, which involves no cooking and is so easy to prepare.

SERVES 4

5 ripe avocados, peeled, 1 finely diced
300ml (^{1}/$_2$ pint) good, strong chicken stock, all fat removed
1 chilli, finely chopped
100ml (3^1/$_2$fl oz) pouring cream
Juice of 2 lemons
8 fresh oysters, shells removed and juice reserved and 4 oysters, chopped
20 chives, chopped
4 teaspoons crème fraîche
1 teaspoon ossetra caviar
Chervil
Salt and pepper

1 Purée the 4 avocados with the stock, half of the chilli, the cream and lemon juice until smooth. Season and chill.

2 To make the tartare, mix the rest of the chilli with the chopped oysters, diced avocado and the chives. Season with salt and freshly ground black pepper.

3 Spoon the tartare into small ring moulds on individual soup plates and pour the soup around it. Remove the ring moulds, and garnish the tartar with the oysters, caviar and chervil.

fish

steamed bamboo **cod** with lemon and braised buttered leeks

Bamboo steamers are wonderful little things. A must in your kitchen. Treat this part of your kitchen equipment well and it will last a lifetime.

SERVES 4

4 cod fillets
3 lemons, sliced
20 baby leeks, washed and
   trimmed
100ml (3½fl oz) chicken
   stock
50g (2oz) butter
4 bay leaves
5 peppercorns
Thyme
Salt and pepper

1 Bring a pot of water to the boil and fit the steamer into it. Steam the fish and lemon for 5 minutes and keep warm.

2 Braise the leeks in the stock with the butter, bay leaf and peppercorns until tender, yet green.

3 Place the leeks by the fish, season and garnish with the lemon, thyme and a bay leaf.

roasted **monkfish** in aubergine skins with red onion, goat's cheese and basil

It's hard to get hold of fresh monkfish these days but when you do, the effort is well worth it. The robust flavours of the fish are complemented by the richness of the goat's cheese and onions.

SERVES 4

2 large aubergines
100ml (3¹/₂fl oz) olive oil
4 x 175g (6oz) monkfish tails
100g (3¹/₂oz) goat's cheese
1 large red onion, cut into
  rings
75g (3oz) basil
Salt and pepper

1   Cut the aubergines in half and, using a small knife, leave about 3mm (¹/₈in) of flesh on the skins, and fry in olive oil until just tender.

2   Place the monkfish in the aubergine skins, and place the goat's cheese, basil and onion on top and season.

3   Wrap snugly in the aubergine skins and roast in a preheated oven at 180ºC/350ºF/ gas 4 for 15 minutes.

crab cakes with kataifi dough and cucumber cream

Kataifi dough is basically shredded filo pastry. It is also known as angel-hair pastry and is often used in Greek, Turkish and Lebanese cooking, especially to make sweet pastry.

SERVES 4

800g (1lb 12oz) fresh crab
   meat
4 egg yolks
20g (³/₄oz) each flat-leaf
   parsley, chervil and dill,
   finely chopped
2 small shallots, minced
1 garlic clove, minced
2 large plum tomatoes,
   skinned, seeded and cut
   into small dice
75g (3oz) butter
500g (18oz) kataifi dough
Vegetable oil
100ml (3¹/₂fl oz) cream
20g (³/₄oz) whole dill leaves
1 large cucumber, half juiced
   and the other, deseeded,
   peeled and finely brunoised
Salt and pepper

1   Mix the crab meat, egg yolks, herbs, shallots, garlic, tomato, salt and pepper and make 8 even-sized balls. Press the balls flat and fry in the butter until golden and all the way warmed through. Place on kitchen paper and keep warm.

2   Pull out and separate the strands of the kataifi dough and deep-fry in vegetable oil and drain well on kitchen paper and season.

3   Bring the cream to the boil and reduce by half. Add the dill and the cucumber juice and gently warm through. Season, strain and add the diced cucumber. Serve with the cakes and pastry.

wild **salmon** with ground polenta crust, watercress, pink grapefruit and poached egg

A fish with a runny poached egg is real comfort food. Although it does not sound that appetizing to some, the taste is truly unique. You simply have to try this combination; the sharpness of the grapefruit spices it up nicely.

SERVES 4

**4 x 175g (6oz) wild salmon
  fillets
Flour for dusting
2 eggs, beaten
50g (2oz) organic polenta
Olive oil
2 pink grapefruits,
  segmented and the juice
  reserved
20 chives, chopped
4 eggs
1 bunch of watercress, leaves
  picked
Salt and pepper**

1 Season the salmon and dust with the flour. Dip in the egg and then the polenta. Fry in a non-stick pan in olive oil for 3 minutes on each side until crispy. Keep warm.

2 Reduce the grapefruit juice; add the segments and season with salt, pepper and the chives. Keep warm in a bain marie.

3 Poach the eggs in boiling salted water. Spoon the grapefruit sauce over the salmon and top with the egg and fresh watercress.

kebabs of **salmon** with yellow pepper, cherry tomatoes, sweet potato and lime butter

Salmon, being firm fleshed, is particularly suited to being skewered though it rarely is for some reason. These kebabs are colourful and tasty – great when the sun's shining.

SERVES 4

**150g (5oz) butter
50g (2oz) dark, brown sugar
4 medium sweet potatoes,
  cut into 2.5cm (1in) cubes
1 medium onion, chopped
1 bay leaf
Small bunch of fresh thyme,
  chopped finely
250ml (9fl oz) dry white
  wine
100ml (3¹/₂fl oz) cream
Juice of 2 limes
800g (1lb 12oz) fresh
  salmon, cut into 2.5cm (1in)
  cubes
24 fresh cherry tomatoes
2 large yellow peppers,
  seeded and cut into 2.5cm
  (1in) cubes
Small bunch of fresh dill,
  chopped finely
50ml (2fl oz) olive oil
Salt and pepper
8 bamboo skewers soaked in
  water**

1 Melt 1 tablespoon of the butter and the sugar in pan and add the sweet potato. Stir until evenly coated, cover and turn down the heat. Simmer until the potato is soft. Keep warm.

2 Place the onion, bay leaf, a little thyme, pepper and the white wine in a pan. Reduce by half, add the cream and the lime juice and bring to the boil. Strain and stir in the rest of the butter.

3 Skewer the salmon, cherry tomatoes, yellow pepper , sweet potato and repeat 3 times. Season with salt, pepper, dill and olive oil. Grill on a hot grill for 2 minutes on each side. Serve with the lime butter.

red snapper stuffed with corn, peppers, prosciutto and purple basil

This is one of my favourite ways to cook fish, and red snapper is also one of the most versatile types of fish available.

SERVES 2

1 large red snapper, gutted
6 cobs of corn, corn cut from the stalk
1 red pepper, seeded and diced
1 green pepper, seeded and diced
8 slices of prosciutto, sliced into strips
1 small bunch of purple basil, leaves picked and chopped, but keeping some for garnish
50g (2oz) unsalted butter
Salt and pepper

1 Mix all the ingredients together except the fish, season and stuff the fish with the mixture.

2 Wrap the fish in tinfoil and roast in a preheated oven at 180ºC/350F/gas 4 for 30–40 minutes or until flaky.

3 Serve on a platter and spoon the juices, and some of the stuffing over the fish and garnish with sprigs of purple basil.

wok-fried **sea bass** with banana leaves and mustard spice

Mustard has been known and used since ancient times, traditionally as a flavouring and even as a medicine. The mustard seed's hot and spicy flavour enhances the gentle taste of sea bass.

SERVES 4

2 tablespoons peanut oil

1 teaspoon yellow mustard seeds

1 teaspoon black mustard seeds

1 medium banana leaf, cut into 5, cut 1 of the sections into 4cm (1.5in) squares

4 x 175g (6oz) fresh sea bass fillets, cut into goujons

Chives, chopped

Salt and pepper

1 Heat a wok until smoking and warm the peanut oil. Add the mustard seeds and then the banana leaf squares.

2 Add the seasoned fish, tossing frequently, until cooked – about 3 minutes.

3 Arrange the banana leaves in separate bowls and divide the fish between the 4 leaves and garnish with chopped chives.

tobacco-flavoured butternut, roasted **swordfish** and beetroot leaves

I do not smoke, but the smell of tobacco, especially cigar tobacco, smells wonderful. I got the inspiration for this when I visited Cuba one vacation. Swordfish is a large game fish with excellent flesh similar to that of tuna. The smokiness of the tobacco lends itself beautifully to the tender flesh of the swordfish.

SERVES 4

4 butternut squash necks, peeled and cut into thick slices, sprinkled with tobacco, wild honey and olive oil, marinated overnight
4 x 200g (7oz) swordfish fillets
4 thyme sprigs
2 lemons, sliced
50g (2oz) beetroot leaves
Olive oil
Salt and pepper

1 Roast the butternut slices with the wild honey in a preheated oven at 180ºC/350ºF/ gas 4 for 20 minutes and cut into neat rounds with a pastry cutter.

2 Grill the swordfish on a very hot grill and roast in the oven at 190ºC/375ºF/gas 5 for 8–9 minutes with seasoning, thyme and fresh lemon slices.

3 Serve the swordfish with the butternut and garnish with the beetroot leaves, which have been tossed in olive oil.

seared **mackerel** with capers, fennel and thyme butter

Mackerel can be used in many ways, but pan searing is quick and it seals in all the goodness and flavour this little fish has. Use plenty of fennel – the aniseed flavour complements the taste and cuts the fattiness.

SERVES 4

1 tablespoon olive oil
4 x 175g (6oz) mackerel
   fillets
2 tablespoons capers,
   drained
4 baby fennel bulbs, thinly
   sliced and kept in
   acidulated water
4 slices of thyme butter
Dill
Salt and pepper

1 Heat a non-stick frying pan and add the olive oil. Cut a few slashes into the skin side of the fish, season and sear on both sides for approximately 2–3 minutes. Keep warm.

2 In the same pan add the capers and fennel, season and cook for about 1 minute and then spoon over the fish.

3 Garnish with slices of thyme butter and dill.

pan seared **sea bass** with salad of beetroot and pear with vanilla bean purée

This is a lovely way to serve sea bass for alfresco dining. Freshness is the most important quality in fish. Fish is rich in vitamins as well as an excellent source of protein; this unusual combination of fresh fish with a fruity salad is an easy and healthy alternative to your average fish and chips.

SERVES 4

3 tablespoons olive oil
4 x 175g (6oz) sea bass fillets,
  trimmed and scored
275g (10oz) white beans,
  soaked for 24 hours and
  cooked until soft
1 vanilla pod, cut in half,
  seeds scraped out and kept
2 garlic cloves, crushed
450g (1lb) mixed salad greens
8 baby beetroots, roasted,
  peeled and quartered
20 chives, finely chopped
2 forelle pears, cut
  lengthways into 8 and kept
  in acidulated water
Chervil
Salt and pepper

1 Heat a non-stick frying pan and add 1 tablespoon of olive oil. Season the fish and fry skin side down for 3 minutes until the skin is crisp and golden brown. Turn over and cook for 2 more minutes until cooked through.

2 Purée the beans with a little water and the vanilla seeds. Warm through and add the garlic.

3 Toss the salad, beetroot, chives and the remaining olive oil and season. Place in the centre of the plates, arrange the pears around and arrange the fish on top. Garnish with quenelles of bean purée and chervil.

octopus with basque-style peppers

I am absolutely infatuated with cooking peppers with tomatoes. Two very basic tastes that are so important and individual, yet a perfect marriage.

SERVES 4

600g (1¼lb) octopus, prepared by a fishmonger
Court-bouillon
Olive oil
2 whole red peppers
4 shallots, finely diced
2 garlic cloves, crushed and finely diced
1 red onion, finely diced
1 green pepper, seeded and finely diced
1 yellow pepper, seeded and finely diced
1 red pepper, seeded and finely diced
1 thyme sprig, leaves picked
2 tablespoons tomato fondue (see page 10-11)

1 Poach the octopus in enough court-bouillon to cover it at 80°C/176°F and then fry in olive oil until golden.

2 Roast the 2 whole red peppers in a preheated oven at 180°C/350°F/gas 4 for about 15 minutes. Remove from the oven and wrap with cling film in a bowl to sweat. Cool, peel and blend it up with a hand blender. Set aside.

3 Sauté the shallots, garlic and red onion in olive oil in a hot pan until translucent. Add the diced peppers and the thyme and cook for 5-6 minutes. Stir in the tomato fondue, blended red peppers and the octopus and simmer for a few more minutes.

roasted turbot on the bone with kumquat marmalade and cep purée

This flatfish has its name written in the history books. Even Napoleon had a turbot dish created in his honour. Its firm and flaky white flesh is delicate and should be cooked very carefully.

SERVES 4

4 ceps
4 turbot fillets on the bone
2 tablespoons olive oil
4 thyme sprigs, leaves picked
5 whole black peppercorns
Kumquat marmalade
15 chives, snipped
Salt and pepper

1 Place the turbot in a roasting tin with the olive oil, half the thyme and seasoning. Roast in a preheated oven at 200°F/400°C/gas 6 for 12 minutes until the flesh starts flaking.

2 Roast the ceps in tinfoil with the remaining thyme and olive oil in a preheated oven at 150°C/300°F/gas 2 for 10 minutes. Purée them in a food processor and warm through on a low heat.

3 Plate the cep purée in the centre of the plate, place the fish on top and garnish with the marmalade and chives.

red snapper with black olives, red onion and tomato

Verjuice is unfermented grape juice. Use white wine as a substitute.

SERVES 2

2 medium-sized red
  snappers, gutted
4 red onions, sliced
4 large plum tomatoes, sliced
2 lemons, sliced
150g (5oz) black olives,
  seeded and chopped
1 bunch of basil, leaves
  picked and chopped
4 tablespoons verjuice
Crusty bread
Salad leaves
Salt and pepper

1 Stuff each fish with all the ingredients, season and drizzle with the verjuice. Any remaining mixture place on top of the fish.

2 Roast in parchment paper in a preheated oven at 180ºC/350ºF/ gas 4 for 20 minutes.

3 Serve them whole with warm, crusty bread and a salad.

lobster with chocolate, cardamom and orange scented milk

A subtle combination of citrus and chocolate spiced up a little with cardamom. Chocolate has been used as a savoury addition to food for a very long time. Make good friends with your chocolatier and he will provide you with special chocolate.

SERVES 4

**250ml (9fl oz) full cream
  milk**
Zest of 1 orange
**2 cardamom pods, toasted
  and crushed**
**50g (2oz) good, dark
  chocolate and a little extra
  for garnish**
4 lobsters
50g (2oz) butter
Orange oil

1   Pour the milk into a small saucepan and add the zest, cardamom and the chocolate. Bring to the boil and then let it simmer for 10 minutes on the lowest heat you have to allow the flavours to infuse.

2   Boil the lobsters in a large pot of boiling water for about 4 minutes, remove and clean the flesh from the shell.

3   Strain the milk, and blend with the butter until frothy. Spoon over the lobsters and garnish with a grating of chocolate and orange oil.

cajun-crusted **yellow tail**, peas and polenta

Yellow tail is part of the tuna family. The pink flesh is best served medium to medium well done. Use blue fin tuna if you can't find yellow tail.

SERVES 4

4 x 175g (6oz) fresh yellow
  tail medallions
2 tablespoons flour, mixed
  with 1 teaspoon Cajun spice
3 tablespoons olive oil
Butter
2 shallots, finely chopped
1 garlic clove, crushed and
  finely chopped
275g (10oz) fresh peas
100ml (3¹/₂fl oz) double
  cream
250g (9oz) polenta
4 lemon wedges
4 thyme sprigs
Salt and pepper

1 Dust the yellow tail with the flour mix, season and fry until crispy in 2 tablespoons of olive oil and butter. Finish off in a preheated oven at 200°C/400°F/gas 6 for 7 minutes.

2 Sauté the shallots, garlic and the peas in the remaining olive oil in a hot pan, add the cream and reduce until thick. Keep warm.

3 Cook the polenta and spoon the peas on top. Arrange the fish on top and garnish with the lemon and thyme.

braised **langoustines** with peppers and tomatoes

Langoustines can be cooked any way you wish. The sweetness of the langoustines balances the acidity in both the peppers and the tomatoes.

SERVES 4

100ml (3¹/₂fl oz) white wine
100ml (3¹/₂fl oz) fish stock
1 carrot, chopped
2 shallots, chopped
1 celery stick
1 garlic clove, finely chopped
1 bay leaf
4 thyme sprigs
16 fresh langoustines
6 ripe plum tomatoes,
  peeled, seeded and cut into
  strips
4 yellow peppers, seeded and
  cut into strips

1 In a roasting tin, bring the wine, stock, carrot, shallot, celery, garlic, bay leaf and thyme to the boil.

2 Add the langoustines and cook, covered with tinfoil, in a preheated oven at 180°C/350°F/gas 4 for 10 minutes.

3 Remove the tinfoil and add the tomatoes and the peppers and cook for another 7 minutes. Serve with the braising liquid.

meat and poultry

braised **pork** fillet with orange and cape malay spice

double **pork** chop with mango and pink pepper

When I came to Cape Town I fell in love with the Cape Malay flavours. The spices are mild and full of flavour.

Pink pepper is the berry of the pepper tree and actually not really pepper. Pepper was used as a currency in the Middle Ages and has become the traditional complement to salt. Ask your butcher to cut the chops for you.

SERVES 4

4 x 175g (6oz) pork fillet
Olive oil
2 carrots, sliced
1 onion, sliced
2 celery sticks, chopped
1/2 head garlic , cloves whole
2 thyme sprigs
1 teaspoon pink peppercorns
3 litres (5 1/2 pints) water
Seasoning to taste
Juice and zest of 2 oranges
1/2 teaspoon each of
   turmeric, marsala, ground
   coriander, cumin
Pinch of ground cloves
Chives
Salt and pepper

1 Seal the pork with olive oil in a hot pan. Transfer to a heavy-based casserole with the carrots, onion, celery, garlic, thyme, half the pink peppercorns and the water. Bring to the boil on top of the stove and season.

2 Cover with tinfoil and place in a preheated oven at 180°C/350°F/gas 4 and cook for 30–40 minutes until done. Strain, reserving the liquid for the pork.

3 Simmer the juice, zest and reserved liquid and reduce by half; add the remaining pink peppercorns and spices. At the last minute add the chives. Place the pork on serving plates and spoon over the sauce.

SERVES 4

4 double pork chops, on the
   bone
2 tablespoons olive oil
1 teaspoon ground pink
   pepper
1 medium mango, peeled and
   cut into julienne
1 teaspoon whole pink
   peppercorns
A few thyme sprigs, leaves
   picked
50ml (2fl oz) sugar syrup
Salt

1 Rub the chops with olive oil, salt and the ground pink pepper. Grill under a hot grill for about 10 minutes on each side, until cooked through.

2 Mix the mango, whole pepper, thyme and the sugar syrup and season with salt.

3 Arrange the chop in the centre of the plate and spoon the mango mixture over the chops.

african braised **oxtail** with cabernet franc, pearl onions and sweet potatoes

Oxtail, once regarded as offal, is now a sought-after rarity and used to make many delicious stews and soups. This dish is based on a South African staple, potjiekos - all cooked in a cast iron pot over a fire.

SERVES 4

2kg (4½lb) oxtail
Olive oil
1 bottle cabernet franc wine
4 thyme sprigs
8 small to medium sweet
  potatoes, peeled and cubed,
25 pearl onions, peeled
Salt and pepper

1 Seal the oxtail in a hot casserole dish in olive oil and add the wine and thyme. Cook in a preheated oven at 150ºC/300ºF/ gas 2 for 2 hours.

2 Add the sweet potatoes and pearl onions and cook for an extra 30 minutes.

3 Season and serve in the casserole dish.

peppered **sirloin** with potato crisps and a parmesan tuille

Steak and chips with a posh twist! The Parmesan biscuit is a stylish garnish.

SERVES 4

4 thyme sprigs, leaves picked
50g (2oz) freshly grated
  Parmesan
2 tablespoons flour
4 large potatoes peeled and
  stored in enough water to
  cover
Vegetable oil
7g (¹/₄oz) white peppercorns
7g (¹/₄oz) pink peppercorns
7g (¹/₄oz) black peppercorns
7g (¹/₄oz) caraway seeds
4 x 175g (6oz) sirloin steaks
Olive oil
Salt

1 Mix the thyme, cheese and flour in a bowl and warm a non-stick pan. Divide the mixture in 4 and sprinkle in the pan to make 4 rounds and cook over a medium heat. Have a shallow bowl of ice water ready and place the pan bottom onto the ice to cool down. Carefully and gently remove the tuilles from the pans and keep on kitchen paper until needed.

2 Slice the potatoes on a mandolin into very thin slices and fry in vegetable oil until golden. Remove from the oil and drain on kitchen paper. Season generously with salt .

3 In a medium-sized pan, toast all the peppercorns and caraway seeds. Finely grind in a spice grinder and mix some salt into it. Rub the sirloins with olive oil and press down into the pepper mix. In a hot non-stick pan, seal the steaks in olive oil and roast in a preheated oven at 200ºC/400ºF/gas 6 for 10 minutes or so, until medium rare. Serve with the chips and a tuille.

thai **beef** salad with egg noodles

I love the flavours of Thai food – refreshing and tangy and crunchy to boot.

SERVES 4

1 red and 1 yellow pepper
1 small bunch of spring
   onions
100g (3¹/₂oz) mange tout
50g (2oz) mung bean sprouts
¹/₂ cucumber, seeded
1 ripe mango
2 red chillies
200g (7oz) dried egg noodles,
   soaked in boiling water for
   5-6 minutes, cooled down
1 small bunch of mint, leaves
   picked and chopped
1 small bunch of coriander,
   leaves picked and chopped
50g (2oz) toasted cashew
   nuts, chopped

For the dressing
2 limes, juiced
50ml (2fl oz) olive oil
1 teaspoon each nam pla,
sesame oil, soya sauce
A pinch of brown sugar
1 small stick (about 2.5cm

(1in) of ginger, peeled and grated
Salt and pepper

600g (1¹/₄lb) loin of beef, cut
   into strips

1   Cut all the vegetables, fruit and 1 chilli into fine julienne. Add half the herbs and the cashew nuts and mix in the noodles.

2   Mix all the dressing ingredients as well as the remaining herbs and the other chopped chilli. Mix well and refrigerate.

3   Sear the beef in a very hot pan with a drizzle of olive oil. Season, cool and add the salad. Dress and serve.

lonely shepherd's **pie**

I use beer with the beef and I also use cubed beef instead of mince. It ends up being dark and rich with plenty of gravy for the mash.

SERVES 4

900g (2lb) cubed sirloin
3 tablespoons flour
2 teaspoons olive oil
350ml (12fl oz) beer
4 large shallots, chopped
4 garlic cloves, chopped
200g (7oz) carrots, sliced
200g (7oz) fresh peas
6 rosemary sprigs, leaves
   picked and finely chopped
500g (18oz) potato mash
Knob of butter
Salt and pepper

1   Dust the beef cubes with the flour and season well. Brown in a hot pan with the olive oil and spoon into individual ovenproof bowls or ramekins.

2   Add the beer, vegetables and rosemary, cover with tinfoil and cook in a preheated oven at 180°C/350°F/gas 4 for 2 hours.

3   Remove the bowls from the oven and then take off the tinfoil and spoon the mash into the ramekins. Dot with butter and brown under a hot grill.

ostrich fillet with sweet potato mash and rum butter

Ostich is now being farmed not only in Africa but in Europe, Australia and America. Buy it fresh. It should have a gamey smell and be dark red.

SERVES 4

250g (9oz) butter
Small bunch of flat-leaf
   parsley, finely chopped
50ml (2fl oz) white rum
4 medium sweet potatoes,
   peeled and cubed
50ml (2fl oz) cream
Knob of butter
4 x 175g (6oz) ostrich fillets
50ml (2fl oz) olive oil
Salt and pepper

1 Mix the butter, parsley and the rum in a food processor until white and fluffy. Roll into a cylinder with some cling film and freeze.

2 Boil the sweet potato in salted water until soft. Drain and return to the pot. Add the cream, some butter and seasoning. Mash and keep warm.

3 Rub the meat with olive oil and season well. Grill on a hot char griller (or griddle pan) until medium rare. Serve with the mash and a slice of the butter.

grilled **rack of lamb** with a cassoulet of leeks, cabbage and bacon

Pinotage is a delicious, South African wine that lends itself perfectly to this dish.

SERVES 4

4 x 175g (6oz) lamb racks
50ml (2fl oz) olive oil
100g (3¹/₂oz) butter, plus a
   few knobs for the lamb
8 rashers of smoked bacon,
   diced
2 large leeks, finely julienned
¹/₂ head of white cabbage,
   finely shredded
200ml (7fl oz) cream
600ml (1 pint) good
   Pinotage wine
Salt and pepper

1 Rub the lamb racks with the olive oil and salt and pepper and place under a hot grill, turning until sealed on all sides. Place in a roasting tin on parchment paper; dot with a few knobs of butter and roast in a preheated oven at 180°C/350°F/gas 4 for 9 minutes.

2 Heat the butter in a pan, add the bacon and the leeks and fry gently until the bacon goes light brown. Add the cabbage and sauté for a few minutes before adding the cream. Simmer over a low heat for 10 minutes and keep warm.

3 Pour the wine into a medium-sized pan and reduce until syrupy. Spoon the cassoulet in the centre of the plate, place the lamb on top and drizzle with the pinotage reduction.

grilled walnut bread filled with spiced **lamb** and red onion marmalade

This is the quickest and easiest midnight snack. Always keep red onion marmalade in your pantry.

SERVES 4

2 loaves of walnut bread,
   sliced in half, but not all
   the way through
4 tablespoons olive oil
4 shallots, finely diced
2 garlic cloves, finely
   chopped
1 chilli, seeded and finely
   chopped
1 teaspoon ground cumin
1 teaspoon ground coriander
4 x 175g (6oz) lamb fillets
4 tablespoons red onion
   marmalade
Rocket, dressed
Salt and pepper

1 Brush the inside of the bread with half the olive oil, fold it open and grill quickly on a hot grill, not letting it burn. Keep warm.

2 In a frying pan, sauté the shallots, garlic, chilli and the spices for 5 minutes in the remaining oil.. Turn the heat up and sear the lamb and season. Roast in a preheated oven at 180°C/350°F/gas 4 for 6 minutes until medium rare. Remove from the oven and let it rest.

3 Fill the bread with some marmalade, sliced lamb and dressed rocket.

roasted rack of **lamb** with jameson lakeshore mustard and minted sourdough

Jameson Lakeshore mustard was a standard addition to Sunday roasts when I still lived at home. I once skipped Sunday school to fetch some from a friend's house to ensure that there was enough for lunch.

SERVES 4

4 x 175g (6oz) lamb racks, trimmed and the bones chinned
4 tablespoons Jameson Lakeshore mustard
Few sprigs of rosemary and thyme, leaves picked and chopped
1 good loaf of sourdough bread
4 tablespoons mint jelly
Salt and pepper

1 Rub the lamb with the mustard, sprinkle with rosemary and thyme and roast in a preheated oven at 180ºC/350ºF/gas 4 for 20 minutes until medium rare. Remove and rest in a warm place.

2 Cut 4 slices of the sour dough and brush with good mint jelly; warm under a hot grill.

3 Cut the lamb in half and arrange on top of the minted sourdough. Drizzle the pan juices on top.

lightly smoked **chicken breast** with chorizo and butter beans

You can build your own smoker, it's great fun. All the goodies you need can be obtained from your local supermarket. Buy the disposable aluminium roasting trays, wood chips and tinfoil for covering.

SERVES 4

4 chicken breasts, with the wing bone on
400g (14oz) cooked butter beans
Chorizo oil
1 chorizo sausage, cut into thin slices, deep-fried and drained
Salt and pepper

1 Build your smoker and heat until it starts to smoke. Smoke the chicken over a low heat for 5 minutes.

2 Season and grill the chicken breasts, turning them once until done and slice into 3. Keep warm.

3 Purée the beans until smooth and warm them well. Place on the plate and arrange the chicken, chorizo oil and chorizo chips around the purée.

stuffed **chicken leg** with corn bread and sage

When stuffing chicken, take great care not to tear the skin. Gently start with one finger and loosen the skin. Keep on wiggling your finger under the skin until it has a 'pocket' large enough to get about a golf-ball size of stuffing in.

SERVES 4

50g (2oz) corn breadcrumbs
25g (1oz) sage leaves, chopped
50g (2oz) soft butter
2 tablespoons fresh lemon juice
50g (2oz) corn kernels
4 portions chicken leg and thigh, skin loosened for stuffing
4 slices of corn bread, cut into rounds with a pastry cutter
2 tablespoons olive oil
Sage leaves, deep-fried
Salt and pepper

1 Mix the crumbs, sage, butter, lemon juice and corn and season. Stuff the chicken leg and roast in a preheated oven at 200°C/400°F/gas 6 for 20 minutes until golden and crisp.

2 Fry the corn bread rounds in the olive oil until crispy on both sides and drain on kitchen paper.

3 Arrange the chicken on top of the corn bread and spoon the roasting juices around. Garnish with the deep-fried sage.

chicken and butternut wanton salad with lemongrass-infused saké

Use the saké as a dipping sauce to add to this wonderful mix of flavours.

SERVES 4

1 stick of lemongrass
200ml (7fl oz) saké
200g (7oz) butternut squash

Salad Ingredients
2 small papayas, peeled,
  seeded and sliced
2 mangoes, peeled and sliced
1 small bunch of coriander,
  leaves picked
6 spring onions, chopped

50ml (2fl oz) olive oil
4 smoked chicken breasts,
  about 100g (3¹/₂oz) each,
  chopped
32 wanton wrappers
1 egg, beaten
150ml (5fl oz) vegetable oil
Salt and pepper

1 Bash the lemongrass with the flat blade of a knife. Add it to the saké. Bring to the boil in a pan, remove from the heat, and allow to cool to room temperature. Strain and reserve.

2 Roast the butternut in a preheated oven at 180ºC/350ºF/ gas 4 for 20 minutes and then mash. Mix the salad ingredients together, season and dress with olive oil. Divide among 4 bowls and set aside.

3 Mix the butternut and the chopped chicken, season and spoon into the centre of each wanton wrapper. Brush with a little egg and pinch the ends together. Fry in the vegetable oil until golden, drain on kitchen paper and serve on the salad.

salad with smoked **chicken**, mango, coriander and white asparagus

White asparagus is more tender, milder and nuttier in flavour than green asparagus and can quickly become your favourite vegetable. This is a fresh salad for summer and spring.

SERVES 4

6 tablespoons rice wine
  vinegar
2 tablespoons olive oil
400g (14oz) salad leaves
1 whole mango, peeled and
  diced
1 small bunch of coriander,
  leaves picked
20 fresh white asparagus
  spears, peeled and blanched
4 smoked chicken breasts,
  cubed
1/2 baguette, thinly sliced
  and rubbed with garlic
Olive oil
Salt and pepper

1 Whisk the vinegar and olive oil and season, pour over the salad leaves and toss well.

2 Mix all the other ingredients, except the bread, with the salad.

3 Fry the bread slices in some olive oil until crispy and golden. Add to the salad and serve.

minoo's fat chick **pizza**

This is a treat: a pizza with such luxurious toppings. Make small bite-sized ones for a cocktail snack, or large ones for watching movies on a cold winter's night.

SERVES 4

2 garlic cloves, crushed and
   finely chopped
900g (2lb) plain pizza dough,
   rolled out into 2 thin bases
225g (8oz) tomato fondue
   (see page 10-11)
200g (7oz) foie gras, cut into
   cubes
110g (4oz) feta, cubed
110g (4oz) grated mozzarella
A few basil leaves
75g (3oz) wild rocket
50ml (2fl oz) olive oil
6 quails eggs
Salt and pepper

1 Sprinkle the garlic on the bases and spread the tomato fondue on each.

2 Top with all the ingredients except the eggs, rocket and olive oil and bake in a preheated oven at 160°C/325°F/gas 3 for 30 minutes.

3 Fry the quails eggs. Toss the rocket with the olive oil and seasoning and add to the pizza with the eggs.

minced **turkey** satay

An American version of shish kebab. If you add a peanut sauce or a chilli jam, it's fusion cooking.

SERVES 4

1kg (2lb 3oz) turkey mince
4 thyme sprigs, leaves picked
1 teaspoon ground coriander
1 chilli, seeded and chopped
Juice of 1 lime
2 tablespoons olive oil
Salt and pepper

Satay sticks soaked in water

1 Mix all the ingredients together.

2 Squeeze the mixture into sausage shapes on the skewers and allow to rest for 2 hours.

3 Drizzle with olive oil and grill on a hot grill until they are cooked through. Serve with chill jam or peanut sauce.

roast whole **duck** with figs and courgettes

This dish should be planned well in advance. Although fairly straightforward, a minimum of 2 hours for roasting is required. Use figs instead of oranges for a surprising variation. If you have too much stuffing add the leftovers to the roasting tray towards the end of cooking time.

SERVES 4

1 whole duck, neck and
  innards removed
2 tablespoons olive oil
6 courgettes, cubed
6 ripe figs, quartered
1 small bunch of thyme,
  leaves picked
Salt and pepper

1 Season the duck by rubbing it with a mixture of olive oil, salt and freshly ground pepper.

2 Mix the courgettes, figs and thyme and season. Stuff the duck with this mixture. Place the duck on a roasting tray in a preheated oven at 180ºC/350ºF/gas 4 and roast for 2 hours.

3 Cut the duck into quarters. Arrange the stuffing on 4 plates. Crisp the duck up under a hot grill, and serve alongside the stuffing and pour over the pan juices.

confit of **duck leg** with star anise and salsify chips

Salsify is also called the 'oyster plant' because of its faint taste of oyster. It is an edible root, white, long and slender.

SERVES 4

Olive oil, enough to cover
    the duck legs
4 star anise
4 duck legs
4 medium salsify roots,
    soaked in water
Vegetable oil

1   Pour the olive oil into a deep roasting tin and add the star anise and the duck legs. Cook, covered in tinfoil, in a preheated oven at 150ºC/300ºF/gas 2 for 1¹/₂–2 hours.

2   Peel the salsify roots with a peeler, cut into chips and deep-fry in the vegetable oil until crisp and golden. Drain on kitchen paper.

3   Remove the duck from the oil and drain well. Serve with the salsify chips.

muscovy **duck breast**, chinese five spice, pineapple and chilli

The Chinese five spice comprises of star anise, cloves, fennel seeds, cinnamon and Sichuan pepper. This combination complements the duck breast very well. The sweetness of the pineapple and chilli adds to the taste sensation.

SERVES 4

4 x 175g (6oz) Muscovy duck
    breasts
1 teaspoon Chinese five spice
1 baby pineapple, peeled,
    quartered and the core
    removed
2 red chillies, seeded and
    finely chopped
Salt and pepper

1   Season the duck breast with the five spice and salt and pepper and sear in a very hot pan, skin side down, until crispy.

2   Slice the pineapple thinly, arrange in a square on a baking tray and sprinkle with chilli and freshly ground black pepper.

3   Place the duck breast on the pineapple and roast in a preheated oven at 200ºC/400ºF/gas 6 for 5 minutes until medium rare.

rare **pigeon** with red onion and focaccia

We used to shoot pigeons as little boys and granny would make the best pigeon pie for lunch. Nowadays, you can buy them farmed, which, unfortunately takes away the game taste. Try and get them wild, even better see if you can hunt them yourself. Ask the butcher to debone them.

SERVES 4

2 medium red onions, diced
1 garlic clove, crushed and
　finely chopped
8 thyme sprigs, 4 with leaves
　picked
50g (2oz) butter
4 slices of focaccia, cut into
　cubes
4 whole pigeon, deboned
150ml (5fl oz) red wine
Salt and pepper

1　Sauté the onions, garlic and thyme in the butter and add the cubed focaccia. Remove from the heat and allow to cool.

2　Season the pigeons and stuff with the bread and onion mix, tying them up well with string.

3　Heat a little oil in a hot pan and seal the pigeons all over and then deglaze with the wine. Place in a preheated oven at 220ºC/425ºF/gas 7 and cook for about 5 minutes. Serve with the red wine as the sauce. Garnish with thyme.

snake beans and **squab** tajines with coconut

Snake beans originate from Asia and are widely used in their cooking. They sometimes grows up to 90cm (2ft 6in) in length and are shaped like snakes.

SERVES 4

4 carrots, finely diced
4 celery sticks, finely diced
4 garlic cloves, crushed
4 large shallots, chopped
4 squabs, quartered
1 litre (1³/4 pints) chicken
  stock
8 snake beans
250ml (9fl oz) coconut cream
2 thyme sprigs, leaves
  removed

1 Place the carrots, celery, garlic, shallots and squabs in the tajine. Cover with chicken stock and simmer for 1 hour.

2 Cook without the lid for 15 minutes until the sauce has thickened and add the beans and replace the lid.

3 Remove the lid, add the coconut cream and garnish with thyme. Tie the beans and use to decorate the squabs.

pasta and risottos

macaroni à la boom boom

This macaroni cheese will surely put some fire in those stormy nights. No fireplace required.

SERVES 4

1kg (2¹/₄lb) macaroni
2 garlic cloves
250ml (9fl oz) smooth cream cheese
250g (9oz) strong, grated Cheddar
250g (9oz) grated mozzarella
100ml (3¹/₂fl oz) fresh cream
4 fresh oregano sprigs, leaves picked and chopped
2 chillies, finely chopped
Salt
Pinch of cayenne pepper

1 Boil the macaroni and the garlic cloves in salted boiling water until half cooked. Drain and tip into a mixing bowl.

2 Mash the garlic and mix in with all the other ingredients, saving some Cheddar to top the macaroni with, and mix with the macaroni.

3 Spoon into a lightly-greased ovenproof dish, sprinkle with cheddar and bake in a preheated oven at 180ºC/350ºF/gas 4 for 10 minutes until the pasta is cooked and the cheese starts going golden brown.

linguine with veal, capers and tomato sauce

The fragrance of capers is spicy and a little bit sour (because of the pickling), the taste is slightly tart and pungent but adds a real tangy taste to this glorifying dish.

SERVES 4

400g (14oz) veal fillets, cut into strips
Olive oil
700g (1¹/₂lb) fresh linguine
1 recipe tomato fondue (see page 10-11)
2 tablespoons capers
2 tablespoons chopped parsley
150g (5oz) Parmesan shavings
Small bunch of basil, leaves picked
Salt and pepper

1 In a hot pan, sauté the veal in a little olive oil with salt and pepper.

2 Cook the linguine until al dente, add the tomato sauce, the capers and parsley.

3 Mix the veal with the pasta, season, and sprinkle with basil and garnish with Parmesan shavings.

pea and **fava bean** risotto

Risotto needs to be eaten straight away – not a dish to make when friends are dropping in 'sometime'! Good quality stock is essential for good flavour.

SERVES 4

100g (3¹/₂oz) butter
1 tablespoon olive oil
1 garlic clove, chopped
2 shallots, finely diced
250g (9oz) Arborio rice
100ml (3¹/₂fl oz) white wine
1 litre (1³/₄ pints) hot vegetable stock
100g (3¹/₂oz) fresh peas, blanched and cooled
125g (4oz) fava beans, blanched and peeled
2 tablespoons double cream
100g (3¹/₂oz) freshly grated Parmesan
20 chives, chopped
Salt and pepper

1 Melt half of the butter with the olive oil in a heavy-based pan over a medium heat. Add the garlic and shallots and stew for a few minutes.

2 Add the rice and the wine and cook until absorbed. Gradually add the stock, stirring and adding more after it has absorbed. Continue until rice is tender.

3 Add the peas, fava beans, the rest of the butter, cream, Parmesan, chives and seasoning.

blue cheese and bacon risotto with rocket and cherry tomatoes

Never 'drown' the rice when making risotto. Adding stock as the rice dries out is the secret of success with this dish.

SERVES 4

100g (3¹/₂oz) butter
1 tablespoon olive oil
1 garlic clove, chopped
2 shallots, finely diced
250g (9oz) Arborio rice
100ml (3¹/₂fl oz) white wine
1 litre (1³/₄ pints) hot vegetable stock
100g (3¹/₂oz) blue cheese
8 rashers of bacon, diced and fried crispy
50g (2oz) wild rocket, washed
100g (3¹/₂oz) cherry tomatoes, cut into half
Salt and pepper

1 Melt half of the butter with the olive oil in a heavy-based pan over a medium heat. Add the garlic and shallots and stew for a few minutes.

2 Add the rice and the wine and cook until absorbed. Gradually add the stock, stirring and adding more after it has been absorbed. Continue until rice is tender and season.

3 Stir in the cheese and the bacon. Garnish with the rocket and tomatoes.

orzo with rocket, pistachio and green papaya

I love the taste of tangy papaya, crunchy pistachios and peppery rocket combined – sublime!

SERVES 4

400g (14oz) orzo

75g (3oz) pistachio nuts, toasted

100ml (3½fl oz) double cream

1 small green papaya, finely diced

2 plum tomatoes, peeled, seeded and diced

15 chives, finely chopped

50g (2oz) fresh rocket, dressed with a little olive oil

Salt and pepper

1 Cook the orzo in boiling salted water until al dente, then drain, rinse and drain again.

2 Mix all the ingredients (including the orzo) together, except the rocket, bring to the boil and season.

3 Spoon the orzo into deep bowls, garnish with the rocket and serve.

penne with alfredo sauce and poached egg

With the poached egg, this dish gets even richer. Fettuccine Alfredo recipes are all slightly varied but have common ingredients such as cream and cheese. This alfredo sauce recipe pays tribute to the classic. If you enjoy pasta give this quick and easy recipe a try.

SERVES 4

100ml (3¹/₂fl oz) cream
Zest and juice of 2 limes
10g (¹/₂oz) thyme, leaves
  picked
4 egg yolks
600g (1¹/₄lb) fresh penne
  pasta, cooked al dente and
  rinsed
4 eggs
150g (5oz) freshly grated
  Parmesan
Olive oil
Salt and pepper

1 Bring the cream to the boil and add the zest, lime juice and thyme.

2 Add the egg yolks and whisk well until the sauce thickens, taking care not to let it split. Add the pasta and season.

3 Poach the eggs and serve on the pasta with the grated Parmesan and a little olive oil.

pappardelle with mustard, cream and crispy spinach

Nowadays spinach is available all year round with the winter varieties having larger leaves. Because of its pronounced flavour, it is either loved or hated. In this recipe we use crispy spinach, adding a different texture to the creamy, smoothness of the pasta. (The photo opposite shows the dish before the spinach is added.)

SERVES 4

10 large leaves spinach, cut
  into juliennes
150ml (5fl oz) vegetable oil
500g (18oz) dried
  pappardelle
50g (2oz) butter
2 shallots, diced
1 garlic clove, chopped
150ml (5fl oz) white wine
300ml (10fl oz) chicken stock
1 tablespoon wholegrain
  mustard
1 tablespoon double cream
4 egg yolks
150g (5oz) freshly grated
  Parmesan
1 tablespoon flat-leaf
  parsley, leaves picked and
  chopped
Salt and pepper

1 Deep-fry the spinach leaves in the oil and then drain on kitchen paper. Cook the pappardelle until al dente. Drain and reserve.

2 Heat the butter in a pan and sauté the shallots and garlic for 2 minutes. Add the wine and bring to the boil, reducing the mixture by half, then add the stock and reduce by half again.

3 Add the mustard, cream and the pappaerdelle and simmer for 3 minutes and season. Add the egg yolks, Parmesan and chopped parsley and garnish with the crispy spinach.

spaghetti with manilla clams, chardonnay, lime and coriander

This dish is quick and tasty. Buy enough clams as you will fall in love with the taste. I've been hooked on it ever since my first bite.

SERVES 4

**100ml (3¹/₂fl oz) good
 Chardonnay
48 fresh Manilla clams,
 rinsed
100ml (4¹/₂fl oz) olive oil
 Zest and juice of 1 lime
1 carrot, diced
2 large shallots, diced
1 fennel bulb, diced
175g (6oz) fresh spaghetti
1 bunch of fresh coriander
Salt and pepper**

1 Pour the wine into a large pan and add the clams. Cover and cook on a high heat for about 5 minutes until the shells have opened. Drain the clams and reserve the liquid. Discard the unopened ones.

2 Return the liquid to the pan and bring to the boil. Reduce by half and add the olive oil and lime zest and juice. Add the vegetables, reduce the heat and simmer for about 5 minutes, or until the vegetables are tender, and season.

3 In a pot of boiling salted water, cook the pasta until al dente and drain. Add the pasta and the clams to the reduced liquid and garnish with the fresh coriander. Serve immediately.

vegetables

polenta tart with herb creamed goat's cheese, confit **plum tomatoes** and watercress

Polenta is really a great product that takes well to any flavour. Venice is where I tasted the best of it. It is a cornmeal porridge that is a traditional dish of Northern Italy. The goat's cheese greatly complements the tomato as well as the sharpness of the watercress.

SERVES 4

2 ripe plum tomatoes, halved
2 garlic cloves, chopped
4 thyme sprigs, leaves picked
Olive oil
250g (9oz) dried polenta
100g (3¹/₂oz) freshly grated
    Parmesan
300g (10oz) goat's cheese
50g (2oz) chopped mixed
    herbs
4 medium-sized ready-made
    pastry cases
50g (2oz) watercress
Salt and pepper
Short crust pastry

1 Place the tomatoes on a baking tray lined with tinfoil, sprinkle garlic, seasoning and thyme on the tomatoes and drizzle with olive oil. Roast in a preheated oven at 60ºC/140ºF for 4 hours.

2 Cook the polenta and then beat in the Parmesan, goat's cheese and herbs.

3 Spoon into the pastry casings, add the tomato, crumble some goat's cheese on top and bake in a preheated oven at 180ºC/350ºF/ gas 4 for 10 minutes or until golden. Garnish with watercress.

pumpkin and spinach **rosti** with goat's cheese

A great dish on a winter's day. This goes well with any plain meat or just a slice of good sourdough.

SERVES 4

4 medium potatoes, par-
  boiled and peeled
1 medium pumpkin, cubed
450g (1lb) baby spinach,
  blanched and chopped
50g (2oz) flat leaf parsley,
  chopped
2 garlic cloves, chopped
Pinch of freshly grated
  nutmeg
150g (5oz) butter
2 tablespoons olive oil
Salt and pepper

1 Roast the pumpkin in a preheated oven at 200°C/400°F/gas 6 for 20 minutes, or until soft.

2 Grate the potatoes and mix with all the other ingredients except the butter and olive oil. Season well.

3 Heat the butter and the olive oil in a medium sized non-stick pan. Place the mixture into the butter and flatten. Turn the heat down and cook until golden. Turn over and do the same. Drain on kitchen paper and serve.

baked baby leeks with bacon, parmesan and **sourdough** breadcrumbs

I love this flavourful combination. Baby leeks have a sweetness that is perfectly complemented by good Parmesan and bacon.

SERVES 4

24 baby leeks, washed and
  trimmed
150 g (5oz) freshly grated
  Parmesan
1 garlic clove, finely
  chopped
1 small bunch of thyme,
  picked
8 rashers of smoked bacon,
  chopped
50ml (2fl oz) olive oil
100ml (3$^{1}/_{2}$fl oz) cream
50ml (2fl oz) white wine
6 slices of sourdough bread
50g (2oz) butter
Salt and pepper

1 Arrange the leeks in an ovenproof dish. Sprinkle the cheese, garlic, thyme and the bacon over the leeks and drizzle with the olive oil.

2 Pour the cream and the wine into the dish and season. Break the bread onto the top and dot with butter.

3 Bake in a preheated oven at 180°C/350°F/mark 4 for 20 minutes until the leeks are soft and the bread is crispy.

red pepper couscous with a basque-style stew of **peppers**

Couscous is a good alternative to rice. This species of pasta, originating in North Africa, can be served with fish or lamb and is even great on its own.

SERVES 4

2 whole red peppers
4 shallots, finely diced
2 garlic cloves, crushed and
   finely diced
1 red onion, finely diced
Olive oil
1 green pepper, seeded and
   finely diced
1 yellow pepper, seeded and
   finely diced
1 red pepper, seeded and
   finely diced
1 thyme sprig, leaves picked
2 tablespoons tomato fondue
(see page 10-11)
300ml (10fl oz) chicken or
   vegetable stock
10g (¹/₂oz) unsalted butter
250g (9oz) couscous
Chives
Salt and pepper

1 Roast the 2 whole red peppers in a preheated oven at 180ºC/350ºF/gas 4 for about 15 minutes. Remove from the oven and wrap in a bowl with cling film to sweat. Let it cool, peel and blend it up with a hand blender.

2 Sauté the shallots, garlic and red onion in olive oil in a hot pan for 1 minute. Add the diced peppers and thyme and cook for 5-6 minutes. Allow to cool and stir in the tomato fondue.

3 Place the stock and butter in a pan, then season to taste and bring to a simmer. Place the couscous in a large heatproof bowl and pour over the stock mixture. Cover with cling film and set aside for 5 minutes, then using a fork fluff up the grains. Stir in the red pepper purée and serve with the hot pepper stew on top and garnish with chives.

rosemary roasted **ceps** with polenta and truffle foam

When ceps are in season, nothing else comes close. Failing which try to use refreshed dried porcini.

SERVES 4

6 large, fresh ceps
8 rosemary sprigs
2 garlic cloves, crushed
2 tablespoons olive oil
250g (9oz) polenta
100ml (3¹/₂fl oz) cream
50g (2oz) freshly grated
   Parmesan
2 teaspoons truffle oil
2 tablespoons cold butter
4 slices of fresh truffle
Salt and pepper

1 Place the ceps, rosemary, garlic and seasoning in a large sheet of tinfoil. Drizzle with olive oil, season to taste and roast in a preheated oven at 180ºC/350ºF/gas 4 for 20–25 minutes until tender. Preserve the juices and keep the mushrooms warm.

2 Cook the polenta and add in a little of the cream and some Parmesan. Adjust the seasoning and keep warm.

3 Bring the roasting juices from the ceps to the boil in a pan and add the rest of the cream, the truffle oil and butter. Blend with a hand blender until foamy. Divide the polenta between deep plates, spoon the ceps on top and garnish with the froth.

sautéed **potatoes** with red onions and yellow tomatoes

Lyonnaise potatoes are potatoes prepared with onions. The yellow tomatoes add colour as well as a crunchy texture. This is a perfect side dish to the roasted monkfish in aubergine (see page 47).

SERVES 4

30 new potatoes, scrubbed, boiled and sliced
Olive oil
4 tablespoons butter
2 medium red onions, thinly sliced
1/2 teaspoon caster sugar
20 baby yellow tomatoes, quartered
50g (2oz) flat-leaf parsley, chopped
Salt and pepper

1 Sauté the potatoes in a hot pan with the olive oil and 2 tablespoons of butter. Season and keep warm.

2 Sprinkle the red onions with caster sugar and caramelise in the rest of the butter in a pan over a medium heat.

3 Spoon the potatoes and then the onions into a bowl. Garnish with the tomatoes and fresh parsley.

green tea soba noodles with mirin **bok choi**, aubergine and sesame seeds

Cooking with green tea gives the ingredients a gorgeous mellow flavour and the sesame seeds ensure this is a crunchy way of using baby aubergines.

SERVES 4

8 baby aubergines, halved
1 tablespoon peanut oil
2 teaspoons white sesame
   seeds
2 teaspoons black sesame
   seeds
4 small heads of bok choi,
   washed and quartered
50ml (2fl oz) mirin
1 tablespoon green tea
250g (9oz) soba noodles
20 cherry tomatoes, 10
   yellow, 10 red
1 tablespoon olive oil
Salt and pepper

1 Brush the aubergines with a little peanut oil, season and grill on a hot grill for 5 minutes on each side. Sprinkle with the sesame seeds and keep warm.

2 Blanch the bok choi and drizzle with the mirin. Season and keep warm.

3 Bring 2 litres (3¼ pints) of water to the boil and add the tea and a pinch of salt. Simmer the soba noodles in the water for 7 minutes and strain. Drizzle with a little olive oil and serve with the whole tomatoes, bok choi and aubergines and season.

baby new **potatoes** roasted with parsley and porcini mushrooms

Add this to any Sunday Roast and watch it disappear.

SERVES 4

200g (7oz) fresh porcini
   mushrooms, sliced
100ml (3½fl oz) olive oil
700g (1½lb) baby new
   potatoes, cleaned
2 garlic cloves, crushed
50g (2oz) butter
4 tablespoons parsley,
   chopped
2 thyme sprigs
Salt and pepper

1 Sauté the mushrooms in a hot pan with a little olive oil. Season and remove from the pan when half cooked.

2 Place the potatoes in a large roasting tin, drizzle with olive oil and sprinkle with salt and pepper. Bake in a preheated oven at 180ºC/350ºF/gas 4 for 30 minutes or until the skin starts to shrivel.

3 Add the garlic, butter, mushrooms and parsley and roast for another 10 minutes.

woked **cabbage** with soya, honey and chilli and egg noodles

This is a deliciously aromatic vegetarian dish that is both tasty and good for you.

SERVES 4

2 tablespoons groundnut oil

1 small red chilli, seeded and chopped

20g (3/4oz) lemongrass, grated

2 small heads of Savoy cabbage

2 small heads of purple cabbage

2 small heads of white cabbage

50ml (2fl oz) soya sauce

50ml (2fl oz) honey

100g (3¹/2oz) egg noodles

Salt and pepper

1 Heat the nut oil in a wok and add the chilli and lemongrass. Fry for a few seconds to release the flavours, then add the cabbage. Wok quickly for 3–4 minutes and add the soya sauce and honey. Toss well.

2 Cook the noodles as pack instructions and add to the cabbage.

3 Cook for a little longer, season and serve.

pepper and mirin roasted baby **carrots** with thyme

People often incorrectly think mirin is a 'rice wine' like saké, but it's actually a Japanese spirit-based liquid sweetener, used only for cooking. It is usually available wherever oriental produce is sold.

SERVES 4

20 baby carrots, stalks on, scrubbed

100ml (3¹/2fl oz) mirin

1 small bunch of thyme, leaves picked

Salt and pepper

1 Place a large sheet of tinfoil on a table with the shiny side up. Fold the edges up and place the carrots inside.

2 Pour the mirin over the carrots, sprinkle with thyme, salt and a generous amount of black pepper. Fold the edges together and seal tightly.

3 Bake in a preheated oven at 180°C/350°F/gas 4 for 10-15 minutes and serve in the foil.

desserts

blackberry cheesecake

Bake a cheesecake with Philadelphia cream cheese and you will be converted. No other cheese gives quite the taste that Philly does!

SERVES 10

For the base
175g (6oz) crunchy biscuits, broken into crumbs
110g (4oz) caster sugar
1 teaspoon allspice
110g (4oz) butter, melted

500g (18oz) Philadelphia cream cheese
1 vanilla pod, seeds scraped out and kept
3 large eggs
110g (4oz) caster sugar
2 tablespoons fresh lemon juice
200ml (7fl oz) blackberry jam, heated
200g (7oz) blackberries

20cm (8in) spring form tin

1 To make the base, combine the crumbs, sugar, allspice and butter and press down onto the bottom of a buttered and lined spring form tin.

2 Whip the cream cheese with the vanilla seeds and add the eggs one at a time, and then add the sugar and lemon juice gradually until well combined.

3 Pour over the crust and bake in a preheated oven at 180ºC/350ºF/gas 4 for 1 hour and cool for at least 6 hours. Pour the warm jam over the cheesecake and add the blackberries before serving.

strawberries with grand marnier and sauce mousseline

I love strawberries. I eat strawberries every day when they are in season. Undoubtably the best and most versatile berry available.

SERVES 4

500ml (18fl oz) water
50ml (2fl oz) Grand Marnier
350g (12oz) sugar
1 star anise
1 vanilla pod, cut in half
400g (14oz) fresh
strawberries, stalks
removed

1 Bring the water, Grand Marnier, sugar, star anise and the vanilla pod to the boil. Add the strawberries and marinate overnight.

2 Blend half of the strawberries with the liquid and pass through a fine sieve.

3 Spoon the sauce into a bowl as well as a spoonful of the whole strawberries and garnish with a vanilla pod, if you like.

rhubarb soup

Rhubarb is a beautifully pink plant mainly used in desserts. Do not eat the leaves as they contain a large amount of oxalic acid. (The photographs show the soup before you garnish with raspberries.)

SERVES 4

1 bunch of fresh rhubarb, leaves removed
350g (12oz) sugar
1 vanilla pod, cut in half
600ml (1 pint) water
Buttermilk sorbet (see page 152)
24 fresh raspberries

1 Carefully string the rhubarb and cut it into 8cm (3 in) sections and blanch for 3 minutes.

2 Bring the sugar, vanilla pod and the water to the boil. Add the blanched rhubarb and purée. Strain and refrigerate.

3 Serve the soup chilled with the buttermilk sorbet and garnish with raspberries.

millefeuille of **nougatine** and fresh berries

An uncomplicated dessert that has a very appealing visual as well as tasty effect.

SERVES 4

200g (7oz) caster sugar
20g (³/₄oz) liquid glucose
110g (4oz) ground almonds
Some vegetable oil for greasing the paper and the rolling pin
2 punnets of fresh, mixed berries
Icing sugar for dusting
4 sprigs of redcurrants

1 Melt the sugar and the glucose on a fairly high heat, stirring all the time until it turns a red-brown colour.

2 Add the almonds and pour onto an oiled baking sheet, roll out thinly with an oiled rolling pin and cut 3 discs per portion.

3 Arrange berries on each but 4 of the nougatine discs. Place them one on top of each other and dust the last one, without the berries, with icing sugar. Garnish with a sprig of redcurrants.

blood **orange** soufflé

To dramatise the presentation you can cut a small slit in the top of the soufflé and pour a tot of Grand Marnier into it. Then, set it alight for a flaming soufflé.

SERVES 4

Juice and zest of 4–6 blood oranges
5 egg whites
50g (2oz) caster sugar
Butter for greasing
Icing sugar for dusting

1 Place the juice and zest of the oranges in a pan over a low heat. Simmer for 5 minutes.

2 Beat the egg whites in a large bowl and gently add the caster sugar. With a metal spoon, fold in the blood orange juice.

3 Butter the ramekins and pour the mixture into them. Cook in a preheated oven at 180ºC/350ºF/gas 4 for 10 minutes until the top has browned and risen, and dust with icing sugar.

vanilla pudding with **prune** compôte

This is a simple pudding that takes no time to prepare and can be made into an elaborate dessert with a topping of compôte or fresh berries.

SERVES 4

200ml (7fl oz) milk
¹/₂ vanilla pod, split lengthways
2 egg yolks
50g (2oz) sugar
15g (²/₃oz) flour, sieved
2 tablespoons cream
Prune compôte

1 Bring the milk and the vanilla pod slowly to the boil in a small pan. Whisk the egg yolks and the sugar together and add the flour while whisking.

2 Slowly pour the milk into the egg mixture while whisking constantly, then pour the mixture back into the saucepan and bring to the boil. Stir constantly while cooking for 3 minutes. Stir the cream in.

3 Strain the mix, refrigerate and serve in glass bowls with the prune compôte.

prune **compôte**

SERVES 4

175g (6oz) prunes, stoned and chopped
4 tablespoons sugar
50ml (2fl oz) cognac
125ml (4fl oz) water

1 Steep the prunes with the sugar in the cognac overnight. Add the water and bring to the boil. Allow to cool or serve hot.

cardamom-scented **oranges**

Serve the oranges hot or cold, in summer or winter. Cardamom is a spice that is widely used in both savoury and sweet dishes, but do not bite onto the seeds. They have a very strong flavour but used properly, they will mesmerise you.

SERVES 4

8 oranges
2 cardamom seeds, toasted and crushed
Buttermilk ice cream (see page 148)
Candied orange zest

1 Peel the oranges and segment them, reserving the juice.

2 Bring the juice to the boil and add the cardamom. Refrigerate overnight and strain.

3 Add the segments to the juice, either warm or cold, and serve with the buttermilk ice cream. Garnish with candied orange zest.

candied orange **zest**

SERVES 4

4 tablespoons water
4 tablespoons sugar
Zest of 4 oranges

1 Bring the water and sugar to the boil and add the zest. Remove from the heat and stir. Use a fork and lift the zest from the sugar and place on a silicon sheet or greaseproof paper. Dry in a low heat oven.

iced **pomegranate** jelly shots

This is a smashing party treat! Have at least 2 per person as they will disappear very fast.

SERVES 2

6 pomegranates (reserve a few seeds for garnishing)

50ml (2fl oz) your choice of alcohol

4 leaves of gelatine, softened in cold water

4 tot glasses

1 Peel and blend the pomegranates and strain the pulp.

2 Mix the pomegranate juice, alcohol and the gelatine until well combined.

3 Pour into the tot glasses and chill. Serve straight from the fridge and sprinkle a few pomegranate seeds on top of each jelly.

Poached **pineapple** with coconut sorbet

Use rum to poach the pineapple. This combination makes me think of the Caribbean. Sunshine and white beaches with palm trees, aahh...

SERVES 4

4 whole baby pineapples
White rum for poaching
4 tablespoons desiccated coconut, toasted
Coconut sorbet

1   Peel and core the baby pineapples and poach in enough rum to cover them.

2   Roll the pineapples in the coconut.

3   Serve in a deep bowl with a little of the rum and a quenelle of coconut sorbet.

spiced pineapple

This is delicious with the vanilla crème brulée on page 147.

SERVES 4

Pinch of Chinese five spice
4 tablespoons maple syrup
1 baby pineapple

1   Peel the baby pineapple, core and cut into thin slices. Heat the spice and the syrup and add the pineapple. Allow to cool off the heat and either dry on silicone sheets or use as is.

warm **apple** crumble

Warm up a cold winter's night with this stunner.

SERVES 4

4 Granny Smith apples,
** peeled, cored and finely**
** diced**
2 tablespoons calvados
3 tablespoons caster sugar
Pinch of allspice
200g (7oz) flour
100g (3¹/₂oz) butter, cubed
** and chilled**
50g (2oz) demerara sugar
Cinnamon ice cream

1 Mix together the apples, calvados, caster sugar and allspice. Spoon into individual medium-sized ramekins and refrigerate until needed.

2 Sift the flour into a bowl and rub in the butter until crumbly. Mix in the demerara sugar and sprinkle over the fruit mixture in the ramekins.

3 Bake in a preheated oven at 180°C/350°F/gas 4 until the crumble turns brown. Serve piping hot.

cinnamon ice cream

A perfect accompaniment to any apple or pear pudding.

SERVES 8

850ml (1¹/₂ pints) milk
1.2 litres (2 pints) cream
350g (12oz) granulated sugar
1 vanilla pod, split, scrapped
** and both seed and pod**
** added to the milk**
¹/₂ teaspoon ground
** cinnamon**
5 large eggs

1 Combine the milk, cream, sugar, vanilla and cinnamon in a saucepan. Cook over a medium heat until the sugar has dissolved – about 15 minutes.

2 Beat the eggs until fluffy and stir in the hot milk mixture taking care not to curdle the eggs. Cook until it coats the back of a metal spoon. Strain into a clean bowl and refrigerate.

3 Churn the ice cream until frozen and freeze.

lemon cake with crème fraîche

I think of the island of Capri when I smell fresh lemons. Whenever I go to the market, I must buy fresh lemons. When I end up with too many I make either this cake, some lemonade or an Asian marinade.

SERVES 8

225g (8oz) unsalted butter
450g (1lb) sugar
4 large eggs
Zest and juice of 8 large
  lemons
350g (12oz) flour
1 teaspoon salt
1/2 teaspoon baking powder
1/2 teaspoon bicarbonate of
  soda
175ml (6fl oz) buttermilk
2 vanilla pods, seeds scraped
  out and kept
250ml (9fl oz) crème fraîche

1 large 25cm (10in) cake
  tin, buttered

1 Cream the butter and the sugar in a bowl until light and fluffy and add the eggs one at a time and the lemon zest.

2 Sift the flour, salt, bicarbonate of soda and the baking powder together. Combine 65ml (2 1/2fl oz) lemon juice, buttermilk and the vanilla seeds in a separate bowl. Add alternately to the still-beating mixture.

3 Pour the batter into the cake tin and bake in a preheated oven at 180ºC/350ºF/gas 4 for 1 hour. Serve warm with the crème fraîche.

coconut rice pudding with exotic fruit

This is a splendid pudding and can be served hot in winter and cold in summer.

SERVES 4

250ml (9fl oz) coconut cream
50ml (2fl oz) double cream
50g (2oz) caster sugar
1 vanilla pod, seeds scraped
  out and kept
50g (2oz) short grain rice
1 kiwi, cut into large dice
1/2 mango, cut into large
  dice
4 strawberries
4 cocktail sticks
100ml (3 1/2fl oz) berry coulis
  (see page 157)

1 Put the coconut cream, cream, sugar and vanilla seeds into a saucepan and bring to the boil.

2 Add the rice and bring back to the boil and simmer for 45 minutes until tender. Cool and then refrigerate until cold.

3 Skewer the fruit onto 4 cocktail sticks, 3 types on each stick, and arrange 2 quenelles of rice pudding on a plate. Spoon over the berry coulis.

grilled **banana** bread with grilled banana

Another of my grandmother's recipes. She could really bake up a storm. The crust of freshly baked banana bread is pure bliss. Add fresh farm butter for a piece of heaven.

SERVES 4

125ml (4fl oz) shortening (use white sunflower vegetable fat)
250g (9oz) sugar
2 eggs, beaten
3 ripe bananas, mashed
500ml (18fl oz) flour
1 teaspoon baking powder
1/2 teaspoon salt
4 teaspoons sour milk
4 extra bananas, sliced, for grilling
4 tablespoons maple syrup
Icing sugar for sprinkling

1 Cream the shortening and add the sugar. Beat well and add the eggs and the mashed bananas.

2 Sift the flour, baking powder and the salt into the mixture and then add the sour milk. Beat until the mixture becomes smooth and creamy. Bake in a buttered bread tin in a preheated oven at 180ºC/350ºF/gas 4 for about 1 hour or until a cake tester comes out clean.

3 Sprinkle the slices of banana bread and banana slices with icing sugar and grill until golden. Drizzle over the maple syrup.

vanilla **crème brulée** with spiced pineapple

Invest in a good blowtorch if you enjoy a good crème brulée. Besides the custard being smooth, the sugar must be caramelised well. When you tap it with the back of a teaspoon you must hear, and feel, a convincing crack. You can serve the pineapple without the spice if you prefer.

SERVES 4

500ml (18fl oz) double cream

65ml (2¹/₂fl oz) caster sugar, plus 8 teaspoons extra for caramelising

4 egg yolks, whisked with the vanilla seeds

1 vanilla pod, seeds scraped out and kept

1 recipe spiced pineapple (see page 139)

1 Combine the cream and the sugar and cook over a medium heat for 5 minutes. Pour the mixture over the egg yolks and vanilla whisked together and whisk until well combined.

2 Strain the mixture and divide among 4 ramekins. Place in a bain marie and cover with tinfoil. Bake in a preheated oven at 150°C/300°F/gas 2 for 30–35 minutes.

3 Cool and refrigerate for at least 3 hours. Sprinkle with the sugar and caramelise with a blowtorch. Serve with spiced pineapple.

charred **peaches** with vanilla ice cream and a drizzle of tequila

A quick and easy dinner party dessert.

SERVES 4

8 very ripe peaches
50ml (2fl oz) tequila
4 scoops of home-made
  vanilla ice cream

1   Char the peaches on a open flame, peel and cut into halves. Catch the juice and keep.

2   Mix the juice with the tequila.

3   Serve the peaches warm with home-made ice cream and drizzle with the tequila sauce.

home-made **vanilla** ice cream

This is so easy to make and definitely worth your while. To make buttermilk ice cream (for page 135) just substitute the cream with buttermilk.

SERVES 8

850ml (1¹/₂ pints) milk
350g (12oz) granulated sugar
1.2 litres (2 pints) cream
1 vanilla pod, split, scrapped
  and both seed and pod
  added to the milk
5 large eggs

1   Combine the milk, sugar, cream and vanilla in a saucepan. Cook over a medium heat until the sugar has dissolved – about 15 minutes.

2   Beat the eggs until fluffy and stir in the hot milk mixture taking care not to curdle the eggs. Cook until it coats the back of a metal spoon. Strain into a clean bowl and refrigerate until cool.

3   Transfer to a freezer, and keep churning the ice cream until all of it is frozen.

caramel trickle ice cream

A simple way to sweeten up your vanilla ice cream.

SERVES 8

1 recipe home-made vanilla
 ice cream
100g (3¹/₂oz) sugar
2 tablespoons water
100g (3¹/₂oz) butter

1 Leave out the vanilla ice cream until soft.

2 Melt the sugar until golden (if you think it's going to burn, slowly add the water) and stir in the butter. Pour over the ice cream.

3 Stir the caramel into the ice cream with the back of a metal spoon and freeze.

grilled exotic fruit salad with planter's punch and mint

Planter's punch is a delicious combination of Jamaican rum, Angostura bitters, fresh lemon or lime juice, Grenadine and soda water. Perfect with exotic fruit.

SERVES 4

1 vanilla pod, seeds scrapped
 out
225g (8oz) caster sugar
20 strawberries, quartered
2 papayas, sliced
4 kiwis, cut into wedges
2 star fruits, sliced
1 mango, cut into wedges
Planter's punch
1 small bunch of mint,
 leaves picked

1 Mix the vanilla seeds with the sugar and dredge the fruit in it.

2 Grill until caramelised and mix together.

3 Serve with the planter's punch and finely julienned mint.

grapefruit and fig gratin

Order this special ice cream from a specialist ice cream shop. They will come up with a recipe. The rosemary and honey ice cream is so lovely, you can eat it just as it is.

SERVES 4

6 tablespoons fructose
3 egg yolks
4 large grapefruit, peeled,
  segmented and juice
  reserved
12 ripe figs, cut across at the
  top and pulled open
Rosemary honey ice cream

1 Mix the fructose, egg yolks and the grapefruit juice together.

2 Place the grapefruit segments in the opened figs and spoon the egg mix over.

3 Gratinate under a preheated grill until golden and serve with the ice cream.

dutch **chocolate** mini cakes

The Dutch are well known for good cocoa. Use only the best and see these little cakes become your favourite snack. This is truly an addictive recipe. Serve with a dark and rich chocolate sauce.

MAKES 30

100g (3¹/₂oz) unsalted butter
175g (6oz) dark chocolate
110g (4oz) caster sugar
2 large eggs
1 vanilla pod, seeds scraped
  out and kept
40g (1¹/₂oz) flour
1 tablespoon Dutch cacao
¹/₂ teaspoon baking powder
110g (4oz) chopped
  macadamia nuts

1 Melt the butter and the chocolate and stir in the sugar. Let the mix cool and then add the eggs and the vanilla seeds.

2 Sift the dry ingredients and stir into the mix together with the nuts.

3 Fill non-stick, miniature silicone moulds or muffin cases and bake in a preheated oven at 180°C/350°F/gas 4 for 10 minutes. Allow to cool and serve with chocolate sauce.

buttermilk sorbet

This goes really well with the rhubarb soup on page 129.

SERVES 8

850ml (1¹/₂ pints) buttermilk
100ml (3¹/₂ fl oz) lemon juice
110g (4oz) caster sugar
500g (18oz) corn syrup

1 Combine all the ingredients, transfer to an ice cream machine and churn.

gianduia mousse cake

Chocolate, chocolate and more chocolate. Gianduia is a smooth mix of ground nuts and chocolate. Turin is the hazelnut capital of Italy and this recipe comes from there. Serve with ice cream or cream.

SERVES 12

225g (8oz) nutella
1 teaspoon hazelnut oil
110g (4oz) butter
250g (9oz) good dark
  chocolate, melted
200g (7oz) milk chocolate,
  melted
6 large eggs
110g (4oz) caster sugar
225ml (8fl oz) cold double
  cream, whipped to soft
  peak

25cm (10in) baking tin,
  buttered and waterproofed
  with tinfoil

1 Stir the nutella, hazelnut oil and the butter into the molten chocolate.

2 Cream the eggs and the sugar until pale and at ribbon stage, then add the chocolate mixture and combine well. Fold in the whipped cream.

3 Pour the cake mixture into the cake tin and bake in a bain marie, in a preheated oven at 180ºC/350ºF/gas 4 for 1 hour. Switch the oven off and let it stand for 50 minutes.

honey **chocolate** cake

One of my chef's in-laws has a private nature reserve on which they grow fynbos. Honey from the fynbos flowers is precious, true liquid gold. It adds character to this chocolate cake. If you can't use this honey obviously use the highest quality you can find.

SERVES 8

175g (6oz) dark chocolate, chopped
75g (3oz) soft butter
2 eggs
6 tablespoons fynbos honey
1 vanilla pod, seeds scraped out and kept
50g (2oz) plain flour
1/2 teaspoon baking powder
1/2 teaspoon salt
Apple sorbet

20.5 x 20.5cm (8 x 8in) buttered cake tin

1 Melt the chocolate and the butter and let it cool. Beat in the eggs, one at a time and then add in the honey and the vanilla seeds.

2 Sift all the dry ingredients together and fold into the mixture.

3 Bake in a preheated oven at 190°C/375°F/gas 5 for 30 minutes and serve with a dollop of apple sorbet.

milk **chocolate** parfait and dark chocolate sauce

The cream prevents the parfait from melting too quickly and also adds to the silkiness of the dessert as a whole. The dark chocolate sauce makes for a beefed up addition to the gentle milk chocolate delight.

SERVES 4

200g (7oz) sugar
75ml (3fl oz) water
8 egg yolks
200g (7oz) milk chocolate, melted
200ml (7fl oz) double cream, and a little extra for the sauce
100ml (3 1/2fl oz) milk
100g (3 1/2oz) dark chocolate

1 Mix the sugar and the water and bring to a temperature of 110°C/225°F/gas 1/4. Pour little by little over the egg yolks while whisking. Whisk until cool.

2 Add the melted chocolate. Whisk the cream and milk until stiff. Fold the egg/chocolate mixture and cream in together and pour into the moulds. Set for a minimum of 6 hours.

3 Melt the dark chocolate and stir in a little cream. Pour large circles of the chocolate sauce in the centre of the plates and place the turned out parfait on top. Garnish with chocolate curls, if you like.

white **chocolate** parfait with marzipan and summer berries

Nuts, berries and chocolate! Great ingredients to use for a summer dessert. The tartness of the berries will balance the sweetness of the marzipan and complement the chocolate parfait.

SERVES 4

200g (7oz) sugar
75ml (3fl oz) water
8 egg yolks
200g (7oz) white chocolate,
  melted
200ml (7fl oz) double cream
100ml (3½fl oz) milk
4 marzipan discs, outside
  diameter of a teacup
Mixed summer berries
Mint

1   Mix the sugar and the water and bring to a temperature of 110°C/225°F/gas ¼. Pour little by little over the egg yolks while whisking. Whisk until cool.

2   Add the melted chocolate and whisk the cream and milk until stiff. Fold the egg and cream in together and pour into the moulds. Set for a minimum of 6 hours.

3   Place a marzipan disc in the centre of a plate and turn out the parfait on top. Garnish with the berries and the mint.

berry coulis

This makes about 250ml (9fl oz) of coulis. Delicious with all types of pudding, or just over ice cream.

100g (3½oz) sugar
100ml (3fl oz) water
½ vanilla pod, cut open
½ star anise
500g (18oz) berries

1   Bring the sugar and the water to the boil and add the vanilla and the star anise. Allow to steep overnight and reheat. Strain and bring to the boil. Add the fruit and allow to cool off the heat. Purée in a blender and strain.

warm flourless **chocolate** cake with chocolate chip cream

The cake comes out gooey and sticky and cheers you up when you are feeling very blue. When you get out of the wrong side of the bed, make this cake and have with lots and lots of the chocolate chip cream.

SERVES 10

4 eggs, separated, whites
   beaten to soft peaks
200g (7oz) caster sugar
200g (7oz) dark chocolate,
   chopped and melted
200g (7oz) butter, melted
200g (7oz) good quality
   chocolate chips
500ml (18fl oz) whipping
   cream, whipped until stiff
   with half the sugar

1 x 25cm (10in) round
   baking tin, lined and
   buttered

1 Beat the egg yolks with half the sugar and combine with the melted chocolate and melted butter.

2 Fold in the stiff egg whites and pour into the baking tin. Bake in a preheated oven at 180ºC/350ºF/gas 4 for about 40 minutes or until the cake tester comes out clean.

3 Fold the chocolate chips into the whipped cream and serve plenty of it with the cake.

index

Apples
   foie gras with Sauternes and apple purée, 17
   warm apple crumble, 141
Asparagus
   salad with smoked chicken, mango, coriander and white asparagus, 84
Aubergines
   green tea soba noodles with mirin bok choi, aubergine and sesame seeds, 118
   roasted monkfish in aubergine skins with red onion, goat's cheese and fried basil, 47
Avocado
   avocado stuffed with prawns, avocado cream and pink grapefruit, 37
   cold avocado soup with avocado and oyster tartare, 41

Bacon
   baked baby leeks with bacon, Parmesan and sourdough breadcrumbs, 112
   blue cheese and bacon risotto with rocket and cherry tomatoes, 101
   grilled rack of lamb with a cassoulet of leeks, cabbage and bacon, 77
Bananas
   grilled banana bread with grilled banana, 144
Beef
   lonely shepherd's pie, 75
   peppered sirloin with potato crisps and a Parmesan tuile, 72
   Thai beef salad with egg noodles, 75
Beetroot leaves
   tobacco-flavoured butternut, roasted swordfish and beetroot leaves, 55
Beetroot
   beetroot and cumin dip with gherkins, 37
   pan seared sea bass with salad of beetroot and pear with vanilla bean purée, 58
   roasted beetroots with crabmeat and curried crème fraîche, 17
Blackberry cheesecake, 125
Bok choi
   green tea soba noodles with mirin bok choi, aubergine and sesame seeds, 118

Bread
   grilled banana bread with grilled banana, 144
   grilled walnut bread filled with spiced lamb and red onion marmalade, 77
Butter beans
   lightly smoked chicken breast with chorizo and butter beans, 81
Buttermilk
   buttermilk ice cream, 134, 148
   buttermilk sorbet, 129, 152
Butternut
   chicken and butternut wanton salad with lemongrass-infused saké, 82
   tobacco-flavoured butternut, roasted swordfish and beetroot leaves, 55

Cabbage
   grilled rack of lamb with a cassoulet of leeks, cabbage and bacon, 77
   woked cabbage with soya, honey and chilli and crispy egg noodles, 121
Caesar dressing, 10
Caesar salad, simple, 33
Cakes
   Dutch chocolate mini cakes, 151
   Gianduia mousse cake, 152
   honey chocolate cake with apple sorbet, 154
   lemon cake with crème fraîche, 143
   warm flourless chocolate cake with chocolate ice cream 156
Capers
   linguine with veal, capers and tomato sauce, 98
   seared mackerel with capers, fennel and thyme butter, 56
Caramel trickle ice cream, 149
Cardamom
   cardamom-scented oranges, 135
   lobster with chocolate, cardamom and orange scented milk, 63
Carrots
   pepper and mirin roasted baby carrots with thyme, 121
Cauliflower and cumin soup with seared scallops, 41
Caviar
   oysters with nori, cucumber, radish and Ossetra caviar, 30
Cheese
   baked baby leeks with bacon, Parmesan and sourdough

breadcrumbs, 112
   blue cheese and bacon risotto with rocket and cherry tomatoes, 101
   drunken pecorino salad with Serrano ham, tapenade and high grown melon, 21
   macaroni à la boom boom, 98
   polenta tart with herb creamed goat's cheese, confit plum tomatoes and watercress, 110
   pumpkin and spinach rosti with goat's cheese, 112
   real French onion soup with Gruyère, 38
   roasted monkfish in aubergine skins with red onion, goat's cheese and basil, 47
   sautéed calf sweetbreads with Gorgonzola and red onions, 34
Cheesecake
   blackberry cheesecake, 125
Chicken
   chicken and butternut wanton salad with lemongrass-infused saké, 82
   lightly smoked chicken breast with chorizo and butter beans, 81
   salad with smoked chicken, mango, coriander and white asparagus, 84
   stuffed chicken leg with corn bread and sage, 81
Chicory
   tempura of prawns, braised chicory, chilli and lime, 26
Chocolate
   Dutch chocolate mini cakes, 151
   Gianduia mousse cake, 152
   honey chocolate cake, 154
   lobster with chocolate, cardamom and orange scented milk, 63
   milk chocolate parfait and dark chocolate sauce, 154
   warm flourless chocolate cake with chocolate chip cream 156
   white chocolate parfait with marzipan and summer berries, 155
Chorizo
   eggs Benedict with chorizo, 18
   lightly smoked chicken breast with chorizo and butter beans, 81
Clams
   spaghetti with Manila clams, Chardonnay lime and coriander, 107
Cinnamon ice cream, 141
Coconut
   coconut rice pudding with exotic fruit, 143
   poached pineapple with coconut

sorbet, 139
   snails stuffed with ginger, lemongrass, coconut and coriander butter, 21
   snake beans and squab tajines with coconut, 95
Cod
   steamed bamboo cod with lemon and braised buttered leeks, 44
Coriander
   salad with smoked chicken, mango, coriander and white asparagus, 84
   snails stuffed with ginger, lemongrass, coconut and coriander butter, 21
Courgette flowers
   stuffed Mediterranean courgette flowers, 33
Courgettes
   roast whole duck with figs and courgettes, 88
Couscous
   red peppered couscous with Basque style stew of peppers, 115
Crab
   crab cakes with kataifi dough and cucumber cream, 48
   roasted beetroots with crabmeat and curried crème fraîche, 17
Cucumber
   crab cakes with katafi dough and cucumber cream, 48
   oysters with nori, cucumber, radish and Ossetra caviar, 30
Cumin
   beetroot and cumin dip with gherkins, 37
   cauliflower and cumin soup with seared scallops, 41

Duck
   confit of duck leg with star anise and salsify chips, 91
   Muscovy duck breast, Chinese five spice, pineapple and chilli, 91
   roast whole duck with figs and courgettes, 88

Eel
   tartare of eel, 29
Eggs
   eggs Benedict with chorizo, 18
   eggs Benedict with Serrano ham and crispy sage, 18
   Minoo's fat chick pizza, 87
   penne with alfredo sauce and poached egg, 104
   truffle scrambled duck egg with

brioche and nut vinaigrette, 34
  wild salmon with ground polenta crust, watercress, pink grapefruit and poached egg, 49
Fava beans
  pea and fava bean risotto, 101
Figs
  figs wrapped in Jambon de Bayonne with ricotta and sugar cane, 14
  grapefruit and fig gratin, 151
  roast whole duck with figs and courgettes, 88
Foie gras
  foie gras with Sauternes and apple purée, 17
  Minoo's fat chick pizza, 87
Frogs legs
  sautéed frogs legs in parsley and ginger butter, 25
Fruit
  berry coulis, 155
  coconut rice pudding with exotic fruit, 143
  grilled exotic fruit salad with planter's punch and mint, 149
  millefeuille of nougatine and fresh berries, 130
  white chocolate parfait with marzipan and summer berries, 155

Gherkins
  beetroot and cumin dip with gherkins, 37
Ginger
  sautéed frogs legs in parsley and ginger butter, 25
  snails stuffed with ginger, lemongrass, coconut and coriander butter, 21
Grapefruit
  avocado stuffed with giant prawns, avocado cream and pink grapefruit, 37
  grapefruit and fig gratin, 151
  wild salmon with ground polenta crust, watercress, pink grapefruit and poached egg, 49

Ham
  drunken pecorino salad with Serrano ham, tapenade and high grown melon, 21
  eggs Benedict with Serrano ham and crispy sage, 18
  figs wrapped in Jambon de Bayonne with ricotta and sugar cane, 14

whole cooked and stuffed red snapper with corn, peppers, Prosciutto and purple basil, 50
Hollandaise sauce, 10

Ice cream
  buttermilk ice cream, 135, 148
  caramel trickle ice cream, 149
  home-made vanilla ice cream, 148
  warm flourless chocolate cake with chocolate ice cream, 156
  cinnamon ice cream, 141
Kumquats
  roasted turbot on the bone with kumquat marmalade and cep purée, 59

Lamb
  grilled rack of lamb with a cassoulet of leeks, cabbage and bacon, 77
  grilled walnut bread filled with spiced lamb and red onion marmalade, 77
  roasted rack of lamb with Jameson Lakeshore mustard and minted sourdough, 78
Langoustines
  braised langoustines with peppers and tomatoes, 64
Leeks
  baked baby leeks with bacon, Parmesan and sourdough breadcrumbs, 112
  grilled rack of lamb with a cassoulet of leeks, cabbage and bacon, 77
  steamed bamboo cod with lemon and buttered leeks, 44
Lemon cake with crème fraîche, 143
Lemongrass
  chicken and butternut wanton salad with lemongrass-infused saké, 82
  snails stuffed with ginger, lemongrass, coconut and coriander butter, 21
Linguine with veal, capers and tomato sauce, 98
Lobster with chocolate, cardamom and orange scented milk, 63
Lonely shepherd's pie, 75

Macaroni à la boom boom, 98
Mackerel
  seared mackerel with capers, fennel and thyme butter, 56
Mango

double pork chop with mango and pink pepper, 68
  salad with smoked chicken, mango, coriander and white asparagus, 84
Melon
  drunken pecorino salad with Serrano ham, tapenade and high-grown melon, 21
Mirin
  green tea soba noodles with mirin bok choi, aubergine and sesame seeds, 118
  pepper and mirin roasted baby carrots with thyme, 121
Monkfish
  roasted monkfish in aubergine skins with red onion, goat's cheese and basil, 47
Mushrooms
  baby new potatoes roasted with parsley and porcini mushrooms, 118
  roasted turbot on the bone with kumquat marmalade and cep purée, 59
  rosemary roasted ceps with polenta and truffle foam, 115
Mussels steamed in mild apple cider with sour cream and oregano, 25

Noodles
  green tea soba noodles with mirin bok choi, aubergine and sesame seeds, 118
  Thai beef salad with egg noodles, 75
  woked cabbage with soya, honey and chilli and crispy egg noodles, 121
Nori
  oysters with nori, cucumber, radish and Ossetra caviar, 30
  three squid rings in nori and polenta dust, 29
Nougatine
  millefeuille of nougatine and fresh berries, 130

Octopus with Basque style peppers, 59
Olives
  red snapper with black olives, red onion and tomatoes, 60
Onions
  African braised oxtail with Cabernet Franc, pearl onions and sweet potatoes, 71
  rare pigeon with red onion and focaccia, 92
  real French onion soup with

Gruyère, 38
  red snapper with black olives, red onion and tomatoes, 60
  roasted monkfish in aubergine skins with red onion, goat's cheese and basil, 47
  sautéed calf sweetbreads with Gorgonzola and red onions, 34
  sautéed potatoes with red onions and yellow tomatoes, 117
Oranges
  blood orange soufflé, 133
  candied orange zest, 135
  cardamom-scented oranges, 135
Orzo with rocket, pistachio and green papaya, 102
Ostrich fillet with sweet potato mash and rum butter, 76
Oxtail
  African braised oxtail with Cabernet Franc, pearl onions and sweet potatoes, 71
Oysters
  cold avocado soup with avocado and oyster tartare, 41
  oysters with nori, cucumber, radish and Ossetra caviar, 30

Papaya
  orzo with rocket, pistachio and green papaya, 102
Pappardelle with mustard cream and parsley, 104
Pasta
  linguine with veal, capers and tomato sauce, 98
  macaroni à la boom boom, 98
  pappardelle with mustard cream and parsley, 104
  penne with alfredo sauce and poached egg, 104
  spaghetti with Manila clams, Chardonnay lime and coriander, 107
Peaches
  charred peaches with vanilla ice cream and a drizzle of tequila, 148
Pears
  pan seared sea bass with salad of beetroot and pear with vanilla bean purée, 58
Peas
  black crusted yellow tail, peas and polenta, 64
  pea and fava bean risotto, 101
Penne with alfredo sauce and poached egg, 104
Peppers
  braised langoustines with peppers

and tomatoes, 64
  kebabs of salmon with yellow pepper, cherry tomatoes, sweet potato and lime butter, 49
  octopus with peppers, 59
  red pepper couscous with Basque style stew of peppers, 115
  saffron broth with pepper stuffed baby squid and green tomatoes, 38
  whole cooked and stuffed red snapper with corn, peppers, Prosciutto and purple basil, 50

Pigeon
  rare pigeon with red onion and focaccia, 92

Pineapple
  poached pineapple with coconut sorbet, 139
  spiced pineapple, 139
  vanilla crème brulée with spiced pineapple, 147

Pistachios
  orzo with rocket, pistachio and green papaya, 102

Pizza
  Minoo's fat chick pizza, 87

Polenta
  black crusted yellow tail, peas and polenta, 64
  polenta tart with herb creamed goat's cheese, confit plum tomatoes and watercress, 110
  rosemary roasted ceps with polenta and truffle foam, 115
  three squid rings in nori and polenta dust, 29
  wild salmon with ground polenta crust, watercress, pink grapefruit and poached egg, 49

Pomegranate
  iced pomegranate jelly shots, 136

Pork
  braised pork fillet with orange and Cape Malay spice, 68
  double pork chop with mango and pink pepper, 68

Potatoes
  baby new potatoes roasted with parsley and porcini mushrooms, 118
  peppered sirloin with potato crisps and a Parmesan tuile, 72
  pumpkin and spinach rosti with goat's cheese, 112
  sautéed potatoes with red onions and yellow tomatoes, 117

Prawns
  avocado stuffed with giant prawns, avocado cream and pink grapefruit, 37
  roasted prawns with piri-piri, 22
  tempura of prawns, braised chicory, chilli and lime, 26

Prunes
  vanilla pudding with prune compôte, 134

Pumpkin and spinach rosti with goat's cheese, 112

Red snapper
  red snapper with black olives, red onion and tomatoes, 60
  red snapper stuffed with corn, peppers, Prosciutto and purple basil, 50

Rhubarb soup, 129

Rice
  blue cheese and bacon risotto with rocket and cherry tomatoes, 101
  coconut rice pudding with exotic fruit, 143
  pea and fava bean risotto, 101

Rocket
  blue cheese and bacon risotto with rocket and cherry tomatoes, 101
  orzo with rocket, pistachio and green papaya, 102

Salad
  chicken and butternut wanton salad with lemongrass-infused saké, 82
  drunken pecorino salad with Serrano ham, tapenade and high grown melon, 21
  salad with smoked chicken, mango, coriander and white asparagus, 84
  simple Caesar salad, 33
  Thai beef salad with egg noodles, 75

Salmon
  kebabs of salmon with yellow pepper, cherry tomatoes, sweet potato and lime butter, 49
  wild salmon with ground polenta crust, watercress, pink grapefruit and poached egg, 49

Salsify
  confit duck legs with star anise and salsify chips, 91

Scallops
  cauliflower and cumin soup with seared scallops, 41

Sea bass
  pan seared sea bass with salad of beetroot and pear with vanilla bean purée, 58
  wok-fried sea bass with banana leaves and mustard spice, 53

Snails stuffed with ginger, lemongrass, coconut and coriander butter, 21

Snake beans and squab tajines with coconut, 95

Sole
  tempura of sole, sesame seed and Mary Rose sauce, 26

Sorbet
  honey chocolate cake with apple sorbet, 154
  buttermilk sorbet, 152
  poached pineapple with coconut sorbet, 139

Soup
  cauliflower and cumin soup with seared scallops, 41
  cold avocado soup with avocado and oyster tartare, 41
  real French onion soup with Gruyère, 38
  rhubarb soup, 129
  saffron broth with pepper stuffed baby squid and green tomatoes, 38

Sourdough
  baked baby leeks with bacon, Parmesan and sourdough breadcrumbs, 112
  roasted rack of lamb with Jameson Lakeshore mustard and minted sour dough, 78

Spaghetti with Manilla clams, Chardonnay lime and coriander, 107

Spinach
  pumpkin and spinach rosti with goat's cheese, 112

Squab
  snake beans and squab tajines with coconut, 95

Squid
  saffron broth with pepper stuffed baby squid and green tomatoes, 38
  three squid rings in nori and polenta dust, 29

Strawberries with Grand Marnier and sauce mousseline, 126

Sweet potatoes
  African braised oxtail with Cabernet Franc, pearl onions and sweet potatoes, 71
  kebabs of salmon with yellow pepper, cherry tomatoes, sweet potato and lime butter, 49
  ostrich fillet with sweet potato mash and rum butter, 76

Sweetbreads
  sautéed calf sweetbreads with Gorgonzola and red onions, 34

Swordfish
  tobacco-flavoured butternut, roasted swordfish and beetroot leaves, 55

Tomatoes
  blue cheese and bacon risotto with rocket and cherry tomatoes, 101
  braised langoustines with peppers and tomatoes, 64
  kebabs of salmon with yellow pepper, cherry tomatoes, sweet potato and lime butter, 49
  polenta tart with herb creamed goat's cheese, confit plum tomatoes and watercress, 110
  red snapper with black olives, red onion and tomatoes, 60
  saffron broth with pepper stuffed baby squid and green tomatoes, 38
  sautéed potatoes with red onions and yellow tomatoes, 117
  tomato fondue, 11, 59, 87, 98, 114

Turbot
  roasted turbot on the bone with kumquat marmalade and cep purée, 59

Turkey
  minced turkey satay, 87

Vanilla
  home-made vanilla ice cream, 148
  pan seared sea bass with salad of beetroot and pear with vanilla bean purée, 58
  vanilla crème brulée with spiced pineapple, 147
  vanilla pudding with prune compôte, 134

Veal
  linguine with veal, capers and tomato sauce, 98

Watercress
  polenta tart with herb creamed goat's cheese, confit plum tomatoes and watercress, 110
  wild salmon with ground polenta crust, watercress, pink grapefruit and poached egg, 49

Yellow tail
  cajun-crusted yellow tail, peas and polenta, 64